CW00742448

An Historical Survey of the

FOREST of DEAN RAILWAYS

Layouts and Illustrations

A Lydney train enters Sharpness Station, circa 1910.

Lens of Sutton

An Historical Survey of the
FOREST of DEAN RAILWAYS

Layouts and Illustrations

Peter Smith

Oxford Publishing Company

ISBN 0–86093–167–6

Typesetting by:
Aquarius Typesetting Services, New Milton, Hants.
Printed in Great Britain by:
Biddles Ltd, Guildford, Surrey

Published by:
Oxford Publishing Co.
Link House
West Street
POOLE, Dorset

ABBREVIATIONS OF RAILWAY COMPANY TITLES

S&W . . . . Severn & Wye Railway
S&WJt . . . . Severn & Wye Joint Line (GWR & MR)
GWR . . . . Great Western Railway
MR . . . . Midland Railway
SWR . . . . .South Wales Railway
FoDCR . . . . Forest of Dean Central Railway
SBR . . . . .Severn Bridge Railway

ACKNOWLEDGEMENTS

I could not have attempted this book without the generous help of many people, foremost among them being Mr Harry Paar, whose own books on the Forest of Dean railways first sparked off my own interest, and which set the standard for all the books that followed. I must also single out, for special thanks, Brian Edwards, who kept coming up with surprises, and Peter Copeland and Mr B. J. Ashworth, who had the foresight to photograph the railways in the area before it was too late. Thanks are also expressed to to Mike Christensen, of the Signalling Record Society, for providing the signalling plans.

I would also like to thank the following people and organizations: Dr A. Dickins, Lens of Sutton, Photomatic, R. Blencowe, C. Maggs, L&GRP, HMRS, D. Ibbotson, H. Ballantyne, T. Shuttleworth, H. Casserley, S. Clarkson and staffs of the Gloucester Records Office and Library. I apologize if any names have been omitted.

Drybrook Road
A nostalgic notice board on the station building.

P. Copeland

BIBLIOGRAPHY

This list identifies the major works available which cover the railways of the Forest of Dean. The first two items are essential reading!

The Severn & Wye Railway by *H. W. Paar* (David & Charles)
The Great Western in Dean by *H. W. Paar* (David & Charles)
Industrial History of Dean by *C. Hart* (David & Charles)
Industrial Tour of the Wye Valley & the Forest of Dean
  by *H. W. Paar* (West London Industrial Archaeological Society)
Steam in the West Midlands and Wales by *B. J. Ashworth* (Ian Allen)
Great Western Branch Line Album by *I. Krause* (Ian Allen)
Great Western Engine Sheds (2 Vols) by *E. Lyons & E. Mountford* (OPC)
Great Western Stations (3 Vols) by *R. H. Clark* (OPC)
The Bristol & Gloucester Railway by *C. Maggs* (Oakwood Press)
A History of the GWR (2 Vols) by *E. T. MacDermot* (GWR)
Great Western Miscellany (Vol. 2) by *J. H. Russell* (OPC)
Railway World, October 1970
HMRS Journal (Vol. 10), pages 96 & 97 and 216 & 217
Railway Magazine, November 1899
Issues of 'Forest Venturer', the Journal of the Dean Forest Railway Society
Items of interest held in Gloucester Library and Records Office

INTRODUCTION

To me, the Forest of Dean was, for many years, a rather mysterious place, seen in the distance from the other side of the River Severn. It was not easy to get at from Dursley, where I was brought up, which increased the aura of mystery, and not until I was older, did the forest glades and walks become more familiar. It was not the Forest itself which compelled me to return so often, but it was a siding at Parkend Station, where the fledgling Dean Forest Preservation Society was based in the old goods shed. From this introduction developed an interest in all the Forest's railways, now all but gone, but once so plentiful. Harry Paar's two books on the lines were invaluable. Without them, I think the area around Bilson Junction would have remained a tangled web in my mind, impossible to unravel, but with the help of these books I gradually got to know all the lines, and the lovely rural area through which they ran.

I hope this book will also serve to unravel the complicated story of the Forest's railways, by taking each line as a separate entity. I have also included the Midland line to Berkeley Road, which could not really be left out, although by no means is it in the Forest. Perhaps, also, the areas potential for modelling will be realized. One can imagine a miniature Lydney Junction, if you have an empty aircraft hanger to spare!

Fortunately, although most of the lines are gone, there is still a ray of hope, for the DFRPS is well established at Norchard, and a visit to the site is an excellent introduction to the Forest of Dean's railways.

Peter Smith
1983

A BRIEF HISTORY OF THE FOREST'S RAILWAYS

The Forest of Dean is an area of wooded upland situated north of the River Severn in West Gloucestershire, bordered, on the west side, by the Wye Valley. To the north and east, it falls away to flatter lowland areas, covering an area of some ten miles from north to south, by five miles from east to west. This small area, today mainly a tourist area, was, at one time, one of the foremost industrial centres in Britain, having extensive deposits of coal and iron ore that have been worked since Roman times.

It was natural that the industries should attract up to date methods of communication, and in the early nineteenth century, three tramroads were opened. Two of these followed the Forest's main valleys, running south to the River Severn. These were the Severn & Wye Tramway, which terminated at Lydney Docks, and the Forest of Dean Tramway, which ran to a dock at Bullo Pill. The third line connected Monmouth with the Forest, joining the Severn & Wye line north of Parkend. These horse-drawn tramroads served the area for many years, but their limitations became more evident in later years, when news of new railways began to filter through from other parts of the country.

The catalyst which brought about the end of the tramways was the opening of the South Wales Railway's main line, in 1851, along the southern fringes of the Forest. In 1854 the SWR took over the Forest of Dean line and converted it into a broad gauge railway, with a northern terminus at Whimsey, near Cinderford. The line was for goods traffic only and was a great improvement on the tramway, but nevertheless the S&W remained a horse-drawn line until 1868, when a single broad gauge line was laid alongside the tramway from Lydney to Wimberry. This was quickly extended to join the SWR, by then taken over by the mighty Great Western Railway. A new line was also opened in 1868, operated by the Forest of Dean Central Railway, from Awre Junction. Built to serve mines in the centre of the Forest, the new S&W mineral loop line took all its potential traffic, and the line was never completed. Operated by the GWR, its existence was something of an embarrassment to Paddington, and it was gradually cut back as traffic failed.

The S&W, meanwhile, prospered, all lines in the area being converted to standard gauge in 1872, and this small company extended its sphere of influence with new lines to Lydbrook, in 1874, and to Coleford, in 1875. Also in 1875, a passenger service began, the first in the Forest, with trains running from Lydney to Cinderford and reversing to Lydbrook Junction, with coaches serving Coleford. A fleet of 0-6-0 tank engines worked the lines, and were based at Lydney Shed.

The next development was in 1879, when the Severn Bridge Railway opened between Lydney Junction and Sharpness, crossing the river by a great viaduct of bowstring girders. Sharpness was the terminus of the Midland Railway branch from Berkeley Road, and an end on connection was made with this line, with S&W trains running through to Berkeley Road and the MR gaining running powers over the S&W. This was later to be important when the S&W was taken over. The SBR eventually became part of the S&W.

A GWR line, from Monmouth, opened to Coleford in 1883, although it only lasted until 1916. It was a victim of the wartime drive for scrap metal and only a stretch of line to Whitecliff Quarry remained until 1967.

The Forest's railway system remained static after this, during a period of industrial decline, culminating in the 1894 take-over of the S&W by the GWR & MR. As a joint line, much of its character remained until the 1960s. Improvements were quickly put in hand, notably a new station at Cinderford in 1900, and a total overhaul of the signalling system. The GWR began a passenger service, in 1907, to Cinderford, from Newnham, on the main line, where a bay was put in. This service also ran to some halts which were opened, north of Whimsey, on the line built in 1883 to Mitcheldean Road, which, until now, was never used. This was an extension of the original 1854 branch on from Whimsey goods station.

The locomotives in the early twentieth century were mainly GWR 0-6-0 saddle tanks of the 2021 class, later rebuilt as pannier tanks, and 517 class 0-4-2 tanks were used on the Forest of Dean branch auto trains. Larger engines were rarely seen, although a 'Dean Goods' was allocated to Lydney Shed.

I will not describe the run down of the system here as this is adequately covered in the plans and detailed notes. Most people will want to visualize the Forest with its railways intact, when this area could pack more railway interest into its confines than any comparable part of Britain. It is to be hoped that someone may be inspired to model some of these lines, as it is through models that some of their former glory may be recreated.

A LIST OF STATIONS AND SIDINGS COVERED BY THE PLANS

The numbers refer to the map, by which each site can be accurately located.

SECTION 1: LYDNEY JUNCTION TO CINDERFORD (S&WR)

 1. Lydney Junction Stations
 2. Lyndey Locomotive Shed
 3. Lydney Docks
 4. Lydney Town Station
 5. Norchard Colliery Siding
 6. Tufts Junction
 7. Whitecroft Station
 8. Parkend Station
 9. Coleford Junction
10. Bisclade Tramway Wharf
11. Speech House Road Station and the Wimberry Branch
12. Serridge Junction
13. Drybrook Road Station and Trafalgar Colliery
14. Cinderford (old) Station
15. Cinderford Station

SECTION 2: LYDNEY JUNCTION TO BERKELEY ROAD (S&WR & MR)

16. Severn Bridge
17. Sharpness Station and Docks
18. Berkeley Station
19. Berkeley Loop Junction
20. Berkeley Road Junction Station

SECTION 3: THE S&WR MINERAL LOOP LINE

21. Crump Meadow Colliery
22. Woorgreen Colliery Siding
23. Lightmoor Colliery
24. Acorn Patch Depot
25. New Fancy Colliery

SECTION 4: THE COLEFORD BRANCHES (S&WR & GWR)

26. Futterhill Sidings
27. Milkwall Station and the Sling Branch
28. Coleford Stations
29. Whitecliff Lime Kiln Sidings
30. Newland Station

SECTION 5: THE LYDBROOK BRANCH (S&WR)

31. Mierystock Siding
32. Waterloo Colliery Siding
33. Upper Lydbrook Station
34. Lower Lydbrook Station
35. Lydbrook Junction Station

SECTION 6: THE FOREST OF DEAN CENTRAL RAILWAY (later GWR)

36. Awre Junction Station
37. Blakeney Goods Station
38. Howbeach Sidings

(For termination of line see plan for New Fancy Colliery; No. 25)

SECTION 7: THE FOREST OF DEAN BRANCH, BULLO TO BILSON JUNCTION (GWR)

39. Newnham Station
40. Bullo Pill Junction
41. Bullo Pill Dock
42. Upper Soudley
43. Staple Edge and Eastern United Colliery
44. Ruspidge Halt
45. Bilson Junction
46. Whimsey Goods Station and Halt
47. Steam Mills Crossing and Drybrook Halts

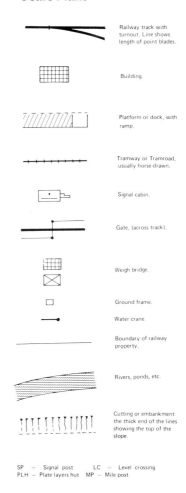

Key To Symbols

Scale Plans

Railway track with turnout. Line shows length of point blades.

Building.

Platform or dock, with ramp.

Tramway or Tramroad, usually horse-drawn.

Signal cabin.

Gate, (across track).

Weigh bridge.

Ground frame.

Water crane.

Boundary of railway property.

Rivers, ponds, etc.

Cutting or embankment the thick end of the lines showing the top of the slope.

SP — Signal post   LC — Level crossing
PLH — Plate layers hut   MP — Mile post

Signalling Diagrams

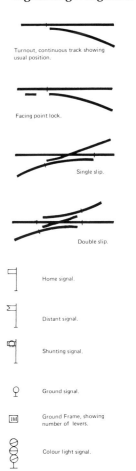

Turnout, continuous track showing usual position.

Facing point lock.

Single slip.

Double slip.

Home signal.

Distant signal.

Shunting signal.

Ground signal.

Ground Frame, showing number of levers.

Colour light signal.

SEVERN & WYE JOINT RAILWAY TIMETABLES (from 1st May 1900)

Station	a.m.	a.m.	a.m.	p.m.	p.m.	p.m.	p.m.	p.m.	p.m.	p.m.	p.m.
Berkeley Road		8.50	10.57	2.10				4.02	6.05	7.25	8.20
Berkeley		8.57	11.04	2.16				4.09	6.11	7.31	8.27
Sharpness		9.03	11.10	2.22				4.15	6.17	7.36	8.33
Severn Bridge		9.08	11.15	2.27			3.45	4.20	6.22		8.38
Lydney Junction (Arrive)		9.15	11.22	2.34			3.50	4.27	6.29		8.45
(Depart)		9.19	11.25	2.36		2.45H	3.57	4.32	6.33		8.46
Lydney Town (Depart)	7.25	9.22	11.28	2.38	2.47	2.48		4.35	6.36		8.48
Whitecroft	7.32	9.29	11.35		2.54	2.55		4.43	6.43		
Parkend (Arrive)	7.34	9.31	11.37		2.56	2.57		4.48	6.45		

Station	a.m.	a.m.	a.m.	p.m.	p.m.
Milkwall	8.00	9.56	11.56	5.06	5.55
Coleford	8.05	10.00	11.58	5.10	5.59

Station	a.m.
Coleford	8.55
Milkwall	8.59

Station	a.m.	a.m.	a.m.	p.m.	p.m.	p.m.
Parkend (Depart)	7.35	9.33	11.39	2.57	2.58	6.46
Speech House Road	7.49	9.45	11.53	3.03	3.04	6.53
Drybrook Road	7.58	9.52	12.00	3.10	3.11	7.00
Cinderford (Arrive)	8.00	9.54	12.03	3.12	3.13	7.02
Cinderford (Depart)	8.10	10.00	12.10		3.16	7.06
Drybrook Road	8.12	10.02	12.13		3.18	7.08
Upper Lydbrook	8.20	10.10	12.29		3.27	7.17
Lower Lydbrook	+	+	+		+	+
Lydbrook Junction	8.26	10.18	12.35		3.33	7.23

+ = Stops when required   H = Thursdays and Saturdays only from 2nd June

GWR ROSS TO MONMOUTH LINE (from 1st May 1900)

Station	a.m.	a.m.	p.m.	p.m.	p.m.
Lydbrook Junction	8.32	10.52	3.12	5.13	7.29
Symonds Yat	8.37	10.59	3.19	5.20	7.35
Monmouth (May Hill)	8.48	11.11	3.30	5.31	7.46

Station	a.m.	a.m.	p.m.	p.m.
Lydbrook Junction	9.53	12.53	3.58	7.42
Kerne Bridge	9.58	12.58	4.03	7.50
Ross-on-Wye	10.08	1.08	4.12	8.00

E = Daily from 1st June

SEVERN & WYE JOINT RAILWAY TIMETABLES (from 1st May 1900)

Station	a.m.	a.m.	p.m.	p.m.	p.m.	p.m.	p.m.
Lydbrook Junction	8.40	11.57	4.02	5.25H		7.45	
Lower Lydbrook	+	+	+	+		+	
Upper Lydbrook	8.48	12.05	4.09	5.33		7.53	
Drybrook Road	8.58	12.20	4.20	5.42		8.04	
Cinderford (Arrive)	9.00	12.22	4.23	5.44		8.06	
(Depart)	9.03	12.25	4.25	5.47	6.10	8.09	
Drybrook Road	9.05	12.27	4.33	5.49	6.12	8.11	
Speech House Road	9.13	12.34		6.19	6.19E	8.18	7.15H
Parkend	9.23	12.42	4.42	6.25	6.25	8.25	7.22

Station	a.m.	p.m.
Milkwall	9.56	9.32
Coleford	10.00	9.36

Station	a.m.	p.m.	p.m.
Coleford	8.55	5.55	9.45
Milkwall	8.58	5.59	9.49

Station	a.m.	a.m.	a.m.	p.m.	p.m.	p.m.	p.m.	p.m.	p.m.
Parkend		9.24			4.43	6.26	7.23	8.26	
Whitecroft		9.28			4.45	6.29	7.26	8.29	
Lydney Town	7.28	9.37	11.22	2.53	4.53	6.36	7.35	8.36	
Lydney Junction (Arrive)		9.40	11.29	2.55	4.55	6.38	7.37	8.40	
(Depart)		9.42	11.34	2.56	5.12	6.41	7.38		
Severn Bridge	7.38	9.49		3.03	5.19	6.48	7.45		
Sharpness	7.45	9.56		3.09	5.25	6.55	7.51		10.08
Berkeley	7.51	10.02		3.15	5.31	7.01	7.57		10.11
Berkeley Road	7.57	10.08		3.20	5.37	7.10	8.03		10.18

+ = Stops when required   H = Thursdays and Saturdays only from 2nd June   E = Daily from 1st June

GWR COLEFORD BRANCH (from 1st May 1900)

Station	a.m.	a.m.	p.m.
Coleford	8.24	12.04	5.29
Newland	8.31	12.11	5.36
Monmouth Troy	8.45	12.25	5.50

Station	a.m.	a.m.	p.m.	p.m.
Monmouth Troy	7.58	9.40	12.55	4.45
Newland	8.12	9.51	1.15	5.05
Coleford	8.19	10.01	1.25	5.15

+ = Stops when required

TIMETABLES FOR STATIONS ON THE EX–GWR GLOUCESTER TO SOUTH WALES LINE
(from 21st September 1953)

	a.m.	a.m.	a.m.	a.m.	a.m.	p.m.	p.m.	p.m.	p.m.	p.m.	p.m.	p.m.
Gloucester Central	4.10	5.50	7.20	9.05	11.10	1.00	1.45	2.10	4.00	5.30	6.15	8.20
Newnham		6.07	7.41	9.26	11.32	1.15	2.06	2.28	4.26	5.50	6.33	8.40
Awre Junction		7.41	7.47	9.33				2.34	4.33	5.56	6.40	8.46
Lydney Junction (GWR)		6.28	8.00	9.45		1.30		2.45	4.45	6.05	6.52	8.58

	Starts here	From Severn Tunnel Junct.	From Cardiff	From Cinderford	From Swansea	From Swansea	From Swansea	From Cardiff	From Cinderford	From Swansea	From Cinderford	From Swansea	From Swansea
	To Cardiff	To Cardiff	To Swansea	To Cinderford	To Swansea	To Cinderford	To Swansea	To Swansea	To Cardiff	To Lydney (not Sats)	To Swansea	To Cinderford	To Cardiff
	a.m.	a.m.	a.m.	a.m.	a.m.	a.m.	p.m.	p.m.	p.m.	p.m.	p.m.	p.m.	p.m.
Lydney Junction (GWR)	7.20	7.53	8.31	9.20	10.33	11.58	1.00	2.55	4.23	5.15	7.02	8.40	12.18
Awre Junction	7.29	8.02	8.40	9.26	10.42		1.10	3.15	4.43	5.30	7.11	8.28	12.47
Newnham	7.35	8.09	8.49	9.20	10.50		1.17	3.23	4.43		7.20	8.28	
Gloucester Central	8.30	8.30	9.07	9.43	11.06	12.24	1.40	3.45	4.45	5.30	7.13	8.45	12.47

GWR FOREST OF DEAN BRANCH TIMETABLES (from 21st September 1953)

	a.m.	a.m.	p.m.	p.m. (S)	p.m. (E)	p.m.	p.m.
Newnham	8.20	11.34	2.08	2.35	3.25	5.50	8.02
Bullo Cross Halt	8.25	11.39	2.12	2.40	3.29	5.55	8.06
Upper Soudley Halt	8.33	11.45	2.19	2.45	3.36	6.01	8.13
Staple Edge Halt	8.37	11.50	2.23	2.50	3.40	6.06	8.18
Ruspidge Halt	8.41	11.54	2.27	2.54	3.44	6.09	8.21
Cinderford	8.45	12.00	2.33	3.00	3.49	6.15	8.28

	a.m.	p.m.	p.m. (S)	p.m.	p.m.	p.m. (S)
Cinderford	9.00	12.40	2.45	4.00	6.30	8.02
Ruspidge Halt	9.05	12.43	2.48	4.03	6.34	8.06
Staple Edge Halt	9.07	12.45	2.50	4.06	6.36	8.13
Upper Soudley Halt	9.11	12.50	2.54	4.10	6.40	8.18
Bullo Cross Halt	9.15	12.54	2.58	4.14	6.44	8.21
Newnham	9.19	1.02	3.07	4.22	6.52	8.28

S — Saturdays only   E — Not Saturdays

The Severn Bridge from the Forest bank.

HMRS

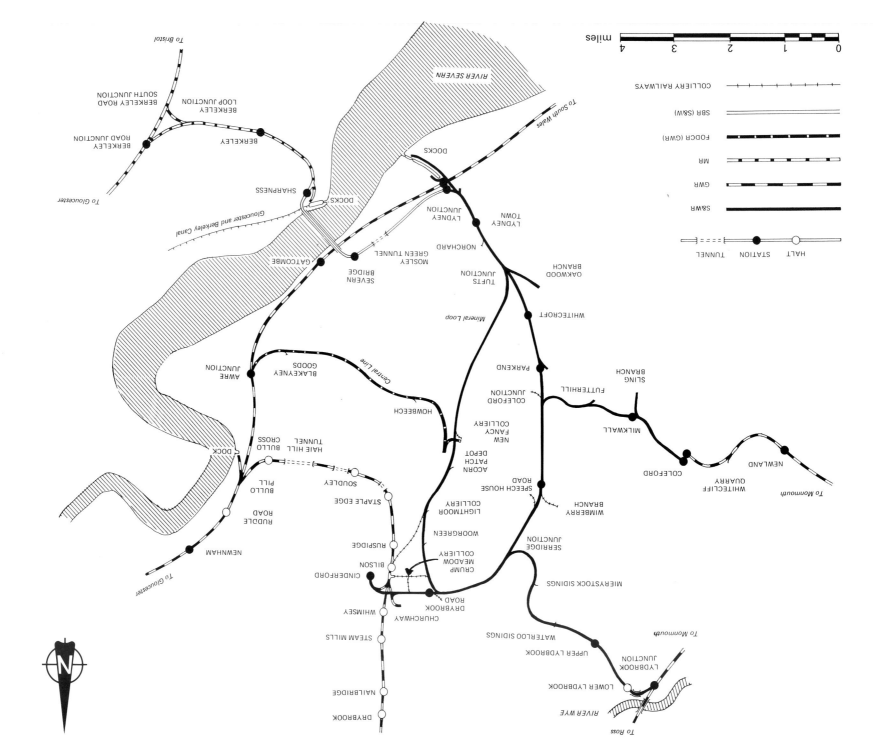

SECTION 1

LYDNEY JUNCTION TO CINDERFORD: SEVERN & WYE RAILWAY

The Severn & Wye line, north of Lydney Junction, replaced the old horse-drawn tramway. In 1868, a broad gauge line was built from the junction to Wimberry, alongside the tramway, with locomotives being used. A depot was built at Lydney to house these locomotives, the first engines coming from Fletcher Jennings & Co.

The opening of the mineral loop, in 1872, between Tufts Junction and Wimberry extended the main line to Drybrook Road, on 22nd April. The main line was mixed until the gauge was made standard on 11/12th May 1872. In 1873, the line was extended to meet the GWR at Bilson Junction, completing the Lydney to Cinderford section in three separate stages. Goods traffic began at once, passenger trains commencing on 23rd September 1875. Until the opening of Cinderford Station, trains reversed at Drybrook Road and continued to Lydbrook Junction.

The S&W main line, as this had now become, flourished until the years between the wars, when the declining industries of the area brought about progressive closure. Passenger trains had been withdrawn on 6th July 1929; the victim of bus competition.

The first closure was from Bilson to Serridge Junction, on 9th December 1951, the goods service having ceased in 1949. Serridge Junction to Speech House Road followed on 21st November 1960 after the closure of Cannop Colliery. Speech House Road to Coleford Junction closed on 12th August 1963 and finally, the Coleford Junction to Parkend section ceased operation on 2nd October 1967. South of Parkend, the line remains, although out of use since 1976. The Dean Forest Railway Society hope to purchase it from British Rail in the near future.

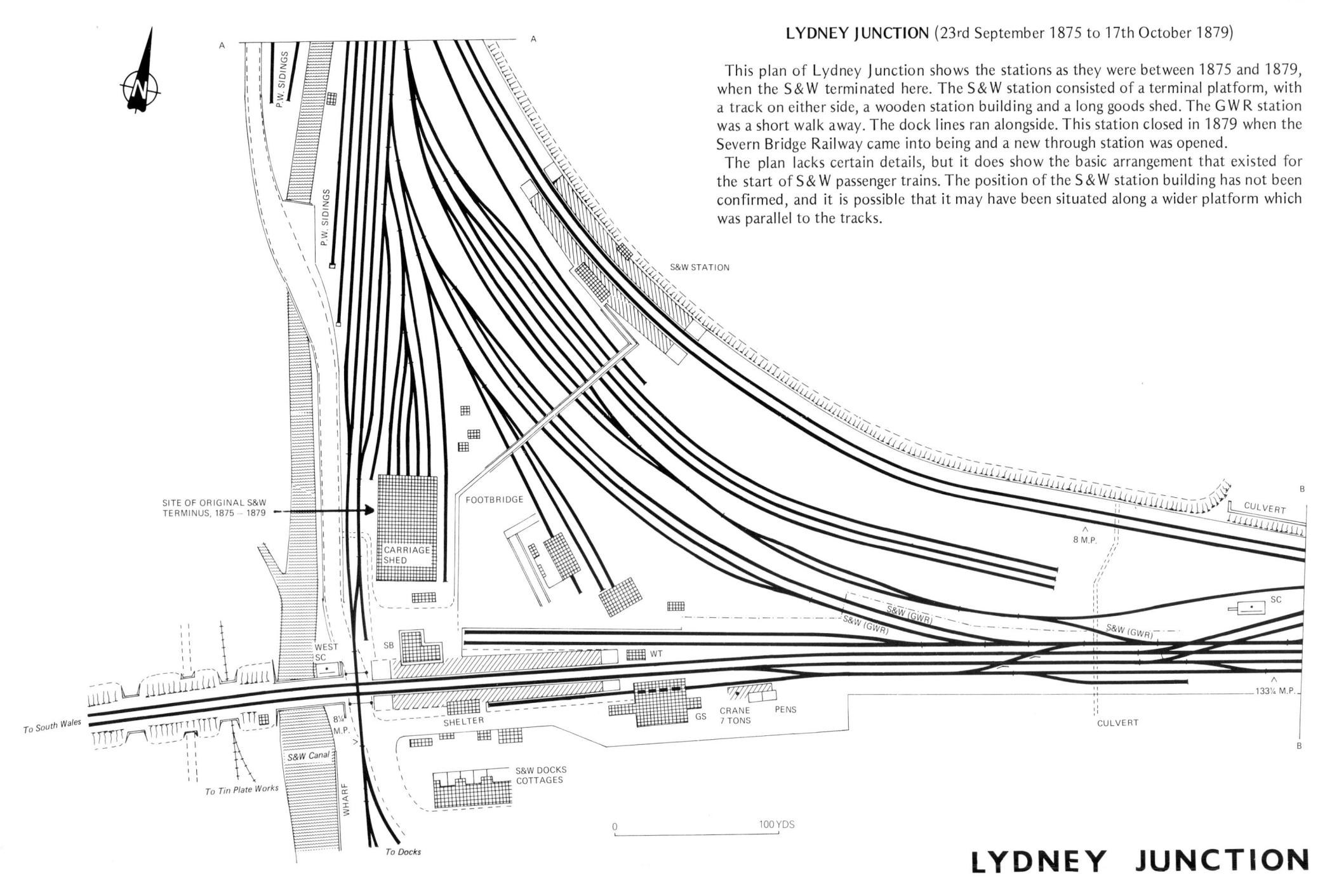

LYDNEY JUNCTION (23rd September 1875 to 17th October 1879)

This plan of Lydney Junction shows the stations as they were between 1875 and 1879, when the S&W terminated here. The S&W station consisted of a terminal platform, with a track on either side, a wooden station building and a long goods shed. The GWR station was a short walk away. The dock lines ran alongside. This station closed in 1879 when the Severn Bridge Railway came into being and a new through station was opened.

The plan lacks certain details, but it does show the basic arrangement that existed for the start of S&W passenger trains. The position of the S&W station building has not been confirmed, and it is possible that it may have been situated along a wider platform which was parallel to the tracks.

A

A

N

P.W. SIDINGS

P.W. SIDINGS

P.W. SIDINGS

S&W STATION

B

CULVERT

8 M.P.

SITE OF ORIGINAL S&W
TERMINUS, 1875 – 1879

FOOTBRIDGE

SC

CARRIAGE
SHED

S&W (GWR)

S&W (GWR)

S&W (GWR)

WEST
SC

SB

WT

133¼ M.P.

To South Wales

SHELTER

GS

CRANE
7 TONS

PENS

CULVERT

B

8¼
M.P.

S&W Canal

To Tin Plate Works

WHARF

S&W DOCKS
COTTAGES

0   100 YDS

To Docks

LYDNEY JUNCTION

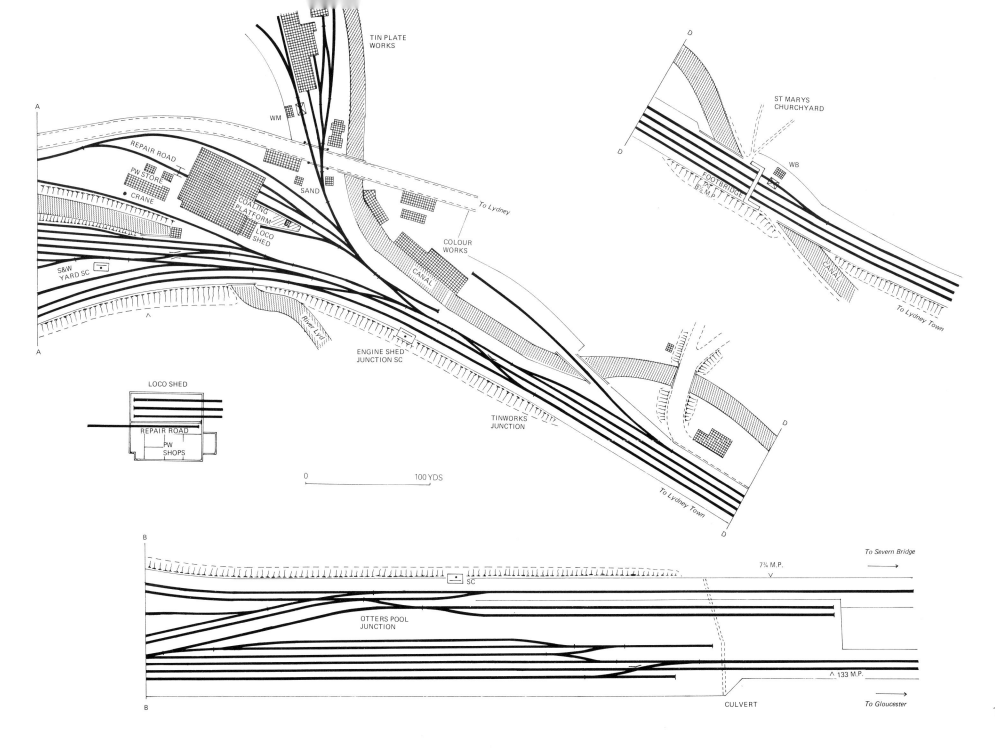

TIN PLATE
WORKS

WM

REPAIR ROAD

PW STORE

CRANE

COALING
PLATFORM

LOCO
SHED

SAND

S&W
YARD SC

To Lydney

COLOUR
WORKS

CANAL

River Lyd

ENGINE SHED
JUNCTION SC

LOCO SHED

REPAIR ROAD

PW
SHOPS

TINWORKS
JUNCTION

0   100 YDS

To Lydney Town

D

ST MARYS
CHURCHYARD

WB

FOOTBRIDGE
8¼ M.P.

CANAL

To Lydney Town

D

To Lydney Town

D

B

To Severn Bridge

7¾ M.P.

SC

OTTERS POOL
JUNCTION

133 M.P.

B

CULVERT

To Gloucester

13

LYDNEY JUNCTION

Opened: (GWR station) 19th September 1851
Opened: (S&W station) 23rd September 1875, as a terminus
17th October 1879, as a through station
Closed: (S&W station only) 1960, due to the collapse of the Severn Bridge. The official closure date was 30th November 1964.
Date of survey: 1920
Date of signalling plan: 1960

The South Wales Railway main line was opened from Gloucester to Chepstow on 19th September 1851 and a station was opened to serve Lydney. The line crossed the Severn & Wye Tramway, on the level, west of the platforms. This arrangement lasted until 1868 when the S&W became a proper railway, and proper interchange sidings were laid, although the crossing remained. Both lines were converted to standard gauge in 1872 and three years later, the S&W opened a terminus station adjacent to, and at right angles to, the GWR station.

This station was closed on 17th October 1879, and a new through station opened to serve the new Severn Bridge line. This new station was approached by crossing a lattice girder footbridge and by following a path from the GWR station. The site of the terminus was used as carriage sidings and a large carriage shed was erected. This shed was, in fact, a second-hand corrugated iron church from Cheltenham!

The contraction of the layout began on 28th June 1960, when S&W yard signal box closed, followed, in 1963, by the closure of the dock branch and level crossing. The S&W passenger service had come to an abrupt halt in 1960 with the damage to the Severn Bridge, although track remained on the branch until 1968. Lydney Junction signal box then closed on 3rd March 1969. Today only the West box remains, as a ground frame, and although the main line station is still open, all the original buildings have gone, and the platforms are now fitted with modern shelters.

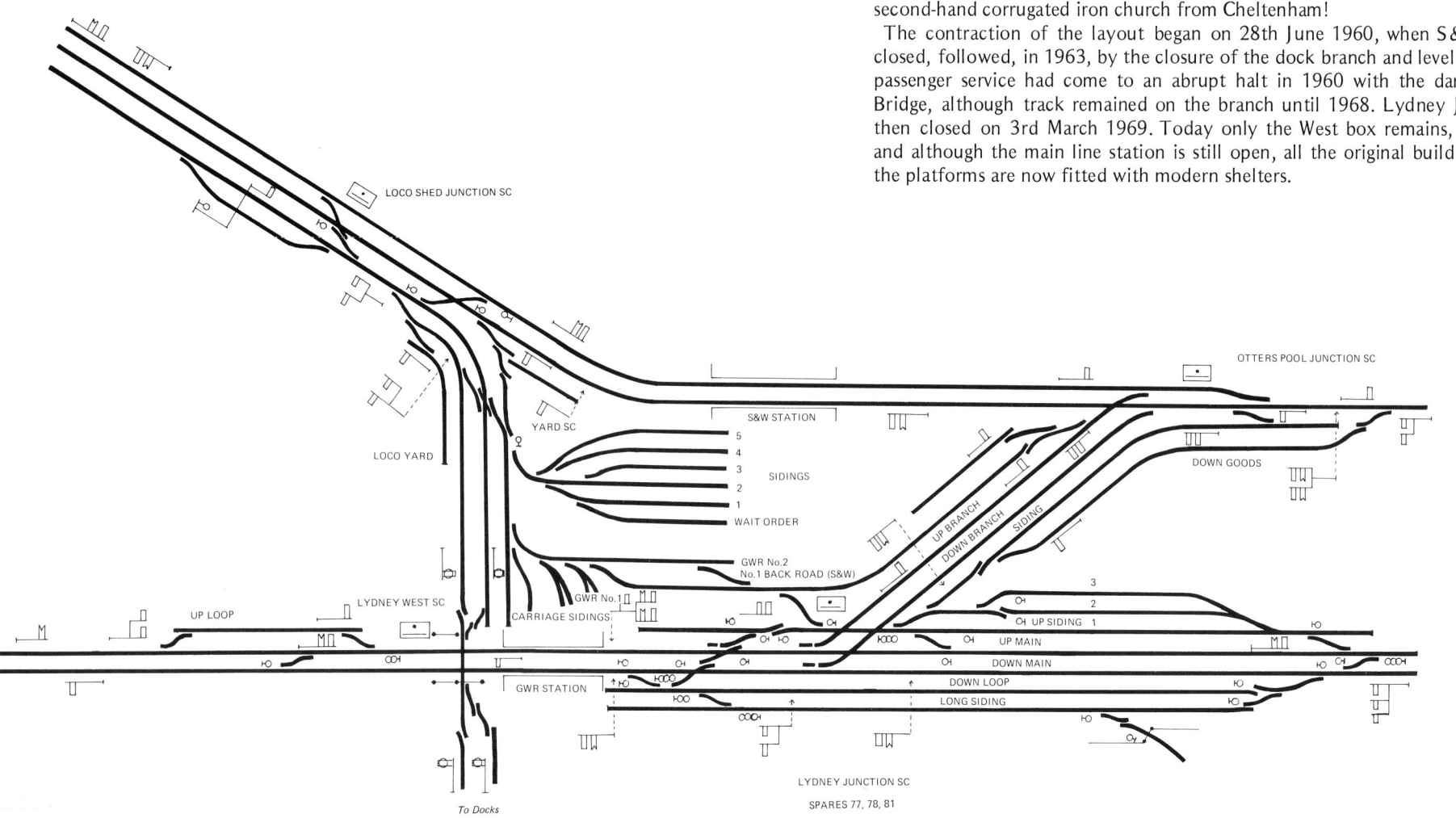

LOCO SHED JUNCTION SC

OTTERS POOL JUNCTION SC

YARD SC

LOCO YARD

S&W STATION

5
4
3
2
1

SIDINGS

WAIT ORDER

DOWN GOODS

UP BRANCH
DOWN BRANCH
SIDING

GWR No.2
No.1 BACK ROAD (S&W)

GWR No.1

UP LOOP

LYDNEY WEST SC

CARRIAGE SIDINGS

3

2

UP SIDING 1

UP MAIN

DOWN MAIN

GWR STATION

DOWN LOOP

LONG SIDING

To Docks

LYDNEY JUNCTION SC

SPARES 77, 78, 81

Lydney Junction
The GWR platforms as seen from the level crossing.

Lens of Sutton

Lydney Junction
The S&W station, looking towards Otters Pool Junction.

HMRS

Lydney Junction
The GWR station, circa 1910, with the S&W carriage shed on the right.

Lens of Sutton

Lydney Junction
A Stanier 2-8-0 locomotive trundles past the GWR goods shed, in 1965.

R. Blencowe

Lydney Junction
An 1890 view, of Otters Pool Junction, with the GWR signal box in the foreground, and the S&W box on the right. Note the early signals with one red spectacle glass, the white being 'clear'.
British Rail

Lydney Junction
The GWR station in the 1950s.

British Rail

Lydney Junction
The S&W station in 1946.

P. Copeland

Lydney Junction
A train for Lydney Town approaches the S&W station in 1946.

P. Copeland

Lydney Engine Shed
The shed, in 1947, with three 2021 class 0-6-0 pannier tanks on view. Note the old coach body.

L&GRP

Lydney Engine Shed
No. 2131 is pictured on shed, in 1947, with a 14XX tank locomotive. The engines are standing outside the running shed.

Lens of Sutton

Lydney Engine Shed
The connection to the main line at Loco Shed Junction, with the MR signal box in view.

R. Blencowe

Lydney Engine Shed
Nos. 4698 and 4624, on shed, a week before closure, on 22nd March 1964.

R. Blencowe

LYDNEY ENGINE SHED

Opened: 1865, as a tramway depot, developing into a locomotive shed between 1868 and 1870.
Closed: 29th February 1964
Date of survey: 1920

Lydney locomotive shed came into being in 1865, when a shed was erected for the engines which were purchased for running on the tramway. It was extended in 1868 to house the broad gauge engines, giving three roads in the locomotive shed and a separate repair shed, served by its own siding. A coaling platform stood outside the shed, with a siding for the wagons. Other buildings included a permanent way store, a crew room and a sand furnace. The main buildings were built of stone, but the later addition to the shed was wooden.

The shed was situated, adajcent to the S&W line, north of Lydney Junction Stations and Engine Shed Junction signal box controlled the entry to the main line. A siding diverged from the shed road to serve Lydney Tin Plate Works, spreading out into an array of sidings. To the north of the shed, the main line ran north, double track, with the mineral line running alongside. At Tinworks Junction, a line ran off to serve a colour works. This line crossed the parallel Severn & Wye Canal.

Lydney Shed, following the take-over of 1894, became host, largely, to GWR engines, these being chiefly 2021 class 0-6-0 saddle tanks. The 1946 allocation showed sixteen 0-6-0 pannier tanks of the 2021 class, two 14XX 0-4-2 tanks and a 'Dean Goods' 0-6-0. The shed closed in 1964 and for the last few years of steam traction, locomotives came from Gloucester Depot.

LYDNEY DOCKS

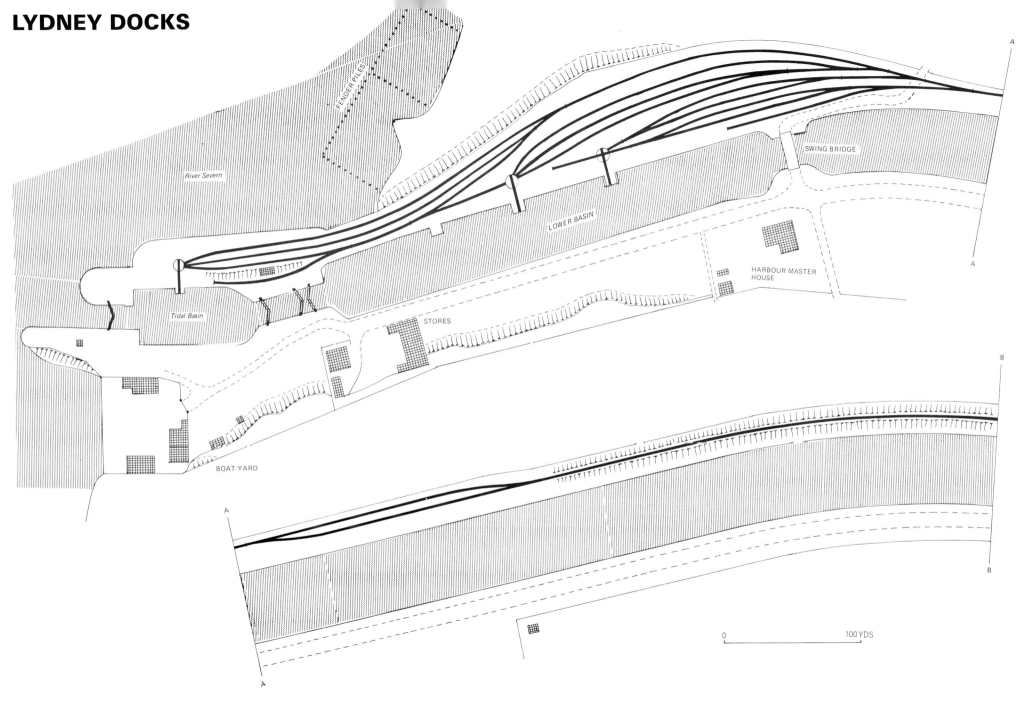

River Severn

FENDER PILES

SWING BRIDGE

LOWER BASIN

Tidal Basin

STORES

HARBOUR MASTER HOUSE

BOAT YARD

A

A

A

A

B

B

A

A

0   100 YDS

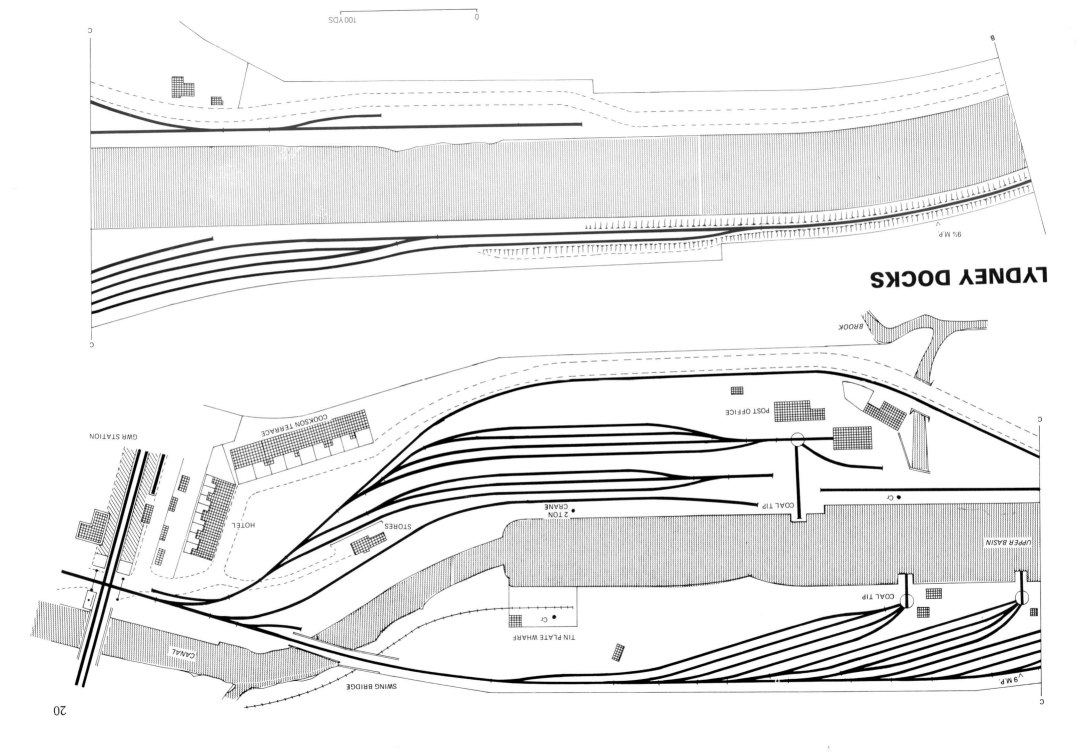

LYDNEY DOCKS

20

LYDNEY DOCKS

Opened: 1813 (Docks); 1868 (Railway)
Closed: 1979 (Docks); 25th August 1963 (Railway)
Date of survey: 1910

The docks at Lydney were formally opened in 1813 as the outlet into the River Severn, for the Severn & Wye Tramway. A canal was also built from the main basin, north, towards Lydney itself. The docks consisted of a short lower basin, next to the inlet locks, and a very long upper basin, which extended as far as the GWR station at Lydney Junction. The tramway, and after 1868, the railway, crossed the GWR on the level, then separated into two branches, serving each side of the main basin. There were many coal tips which produced the main outgoing traffic. Coal was sailed to, among other places, Newport, Bristol, Bridgwater, Minehead and Ilfracombe. Other items handled included china clay, stone and agricultural implements.

The dock declined in the 20th century, losing trade to Sharpness, reflecting the fortunes of the Forest's industries. The railway to the docks was closed on 25th August 1963 and the last revenue-earning ship called in 1979. There remain many items of interest, including a building dated 1813 and the cottages, built by the S&W, to house its workers.

LYDNEY TOWN

Opened: 23rd September 1875
Closed: 26th October 1960 (to passengers); 2nd October 1967 (to freight)
Date of survey: 1920
Date of signalling plan: 1960

Lydney Town was a busy station, convenient for the town, and it retained its passenger service long after most S&W stations had closed. Opened in 1875, for the start of the passenger service, the station was south of the level crossing on the A48 road, having two platforms with the usual small wooden building and a wooden signal box on the 'up' platform.

When the S&W was taken over in 1894, improvements were quickly made to the station by the GWR. In 1896, a new station building was built, together with a metal footbridge and a new 31 lever signal box, next to the crossing. The old S&W box was moved to Serridge Junction. A siding served Watts Brewery until July 1933, while the small goods yard, west of the main line, served cattle pens and a small wooden goods shed. North of the level crossing further sidings diverged, serving various private companies.

After 1929, Lydney Town was the terminus for the passenger service from Berkeley Road. Auto trains were introduced in 1936, as when locomotives were required to run round their trains, the level crossing had to be closed. The auto trains continued until 1960, when the service was interrupted, on 26 October, by the damage to the Severn Bridge. It was never restored and the station closed as from that date. The last sidings were removed in 1967 and the signal box was closed on 2nd October 1967. The site has now been cleared.

Lydney Town
The GWR signal box, as seen from the level crossing, in the 1960s.

Lens of Sutton

Lydney Town
No. 1413 on a Berkeley Road train in the late 1950s. The original S&W buildings are on the left.

Photomatic

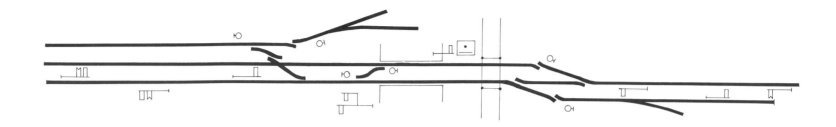

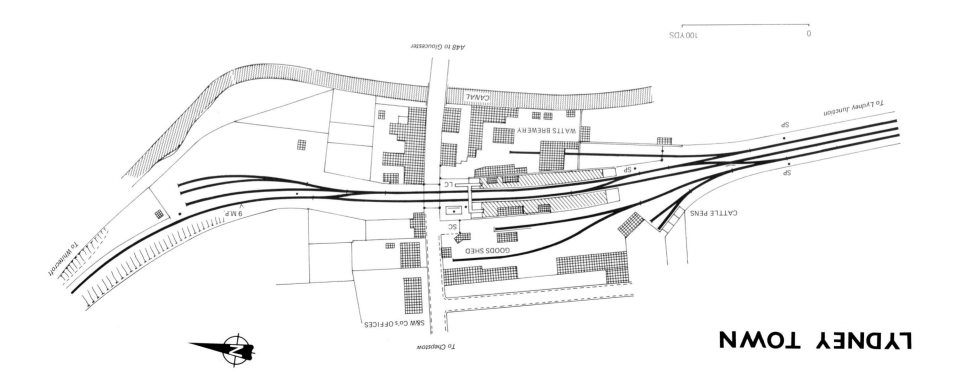

LYDNEY TOWN

To Whitecroft

9 M.P.

A48 to Gloucester

CANAL

WATTS BREWERY

S&W Co's OFFICES

To Chepstow

LC

SC

GOODS SHED

CATTLE PENS

SP

SP

SP

To Lydney Junction

0   100 YDS

Lydney Town
Looking north from the main building, showing the station canopy in detail.

P. Copeland

Lydney Town
The station, looking north, in the 1950s.

Lens of Sutton

Lydney Town
The main platform, as seen after 1896, with all GWR buildings. This view dates from the 1960s when the footbridge had been removed.

Lens of Sutton

Lydney Town
An auto train from Berkeley Road, showing the Hawksworth trailer which was designated for use on this line.

Lens of Sutton

Lydney Town
The original S&W buildings, with the brewery beyond.

Lens of Sutton

Lydney Town
The station, circa 1900, soon after additions were made by the GWR.
Lens of Sutton

Opened: 1906
Closed: 31st December 1960
Date of survey: 1925

The original siding, serving Norchard Colliery, known as Kidnalls Siding, was situated to the north of the connections which are described here. The pit, owned by Park Colliery Co. Ltd., was, by Forest standards, a large producer of coal. In 1923, the West Gloucestershire Power Station opened on an adjacent site, and at once, much of the colliery's production was transferred to the power-station. The new sidings were put in during 1906, although later, a great deal of coal went to the power-station by conveyer belt. The southern connection was removed on 4th January 1948 and things remained static until the closure of the power-station in 1957. The power-station had supported the colliery, and the pit, at once, ceased production, being uneconomical in terms of ordinary coal production. The rail connection remained until 1960 and soon afterwards, the whole site was cleared and left derelict.

In 1978, the colliery site was taken over by the Dean Forest Railway Society, and now a flourishing steam centre has been established, preserving a small part of the Forest's railways.

A wagon of the Gloucester Railway Carriage & Wagon Co. Ltd., which was built in April 1901. The livery is lead grey, and it is lettered in white, shaded black, with black ironwork.

OPC Collection

A wagon of the Gloucester Railway Carriage & Wagon Co. Ltd., which was built in December 1912. The livery is lead grey, and it is lettered in white with black ironwork. The small lettering reads 'Empty to Norchard Colliery, S & W Jt. Rly.'.

OPC Collection

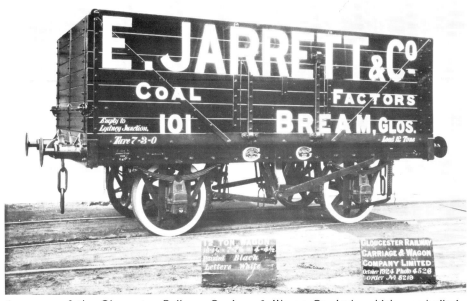

A wagon of the Gloucester Railway Carriage & Wagon Co. Ltd., which was built in October 1924. The livery is black, and it is lettered in white.

OPC Collection

NORCHARD

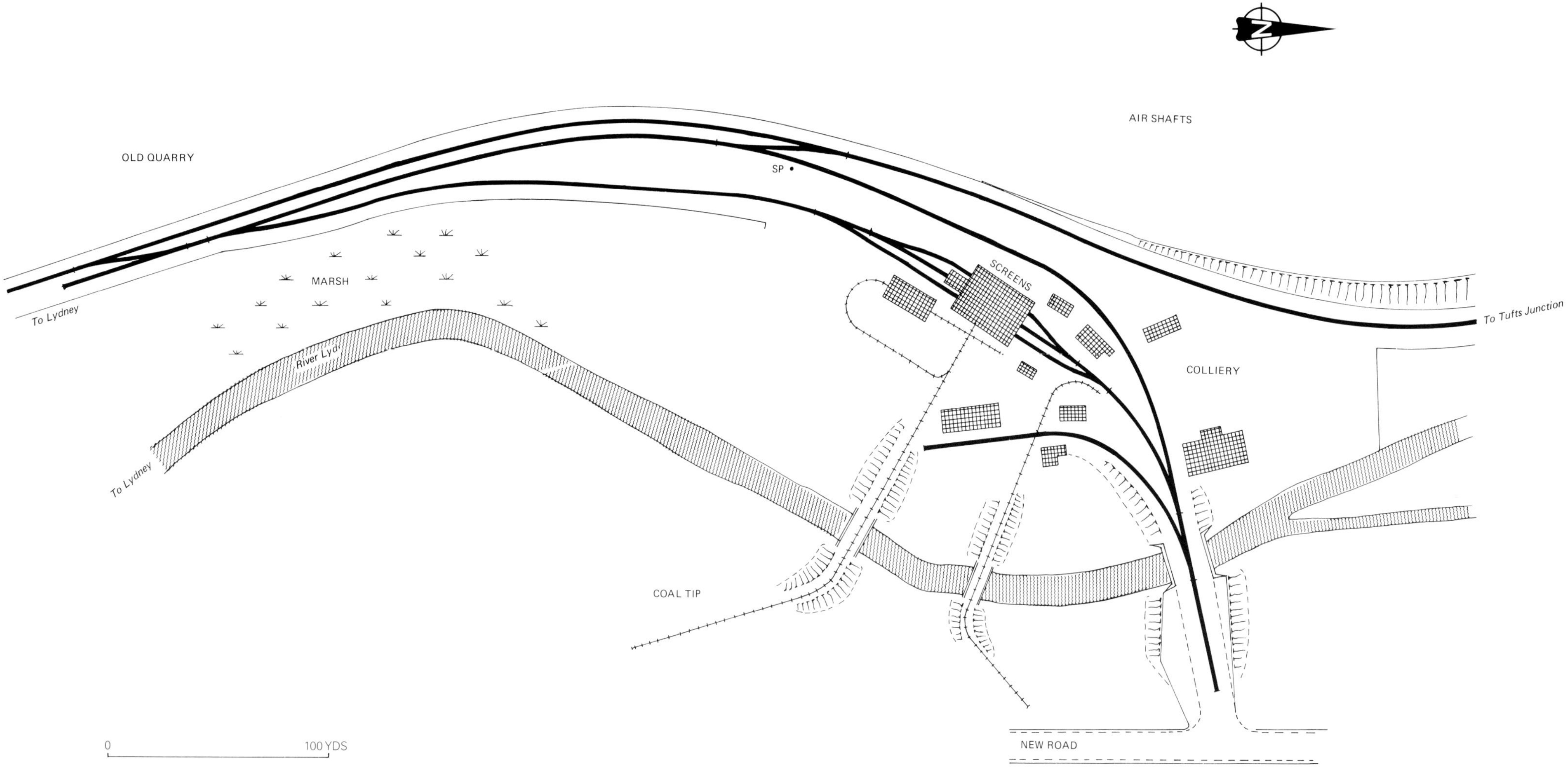

OLD QUARRY

AIR SHAFTS

SP •

MARSH

To Lydney

River Lyd

SCREENS

To Tufts Junction

COLLIERY

To Lydney

COAL TIP

NEW ROAD

0   100 YDS

Tufts Junction
A coal train comes off the Princess Royal branch behind pannier tank No. 9619.

R. Blencowe

TUFTS JUNCTION

Opened: 1868
Closed: 2nd October 1967 (signal box)
Date of survey: 1920
Date of signalling plan: 1955

Tufts Junction was situated in a lovely part of the Lyd Valley, with steep wooded slopes on all sides. It came into being when the S&W line became a railway in 1868, at first being the junction for the Oakwood mineral branch, which served Whitecroft Level and Parkhill Level mines. It was later extended to the large Princess Royal Colliery, while sidings served the Lydney Park Ironworks just beyond the junction.

The junction became more important with the opening of the mineral loop line, on 22nd April 1872. This loop diverged here to run north-east to Drybrook Road, serving many mines on the way. After 1896, the junction was controlled from a small GWR signal box, situated where the Oakwood branch joined the main line.

After a period of disuse, the mineral loop at the junction was removed in October 1959, after its closure in 1957. The Oakwood line closed on 16th February 1965, and with only the single main line track remaining the signal box closed on 2nd October 1967.

A wagon of the Gloucester Railway Carriage & Wagon Co. Ltd., which was built in January 1897. The livery is red with white lettering shaded in black. It has black ironwork.

OPC Collection

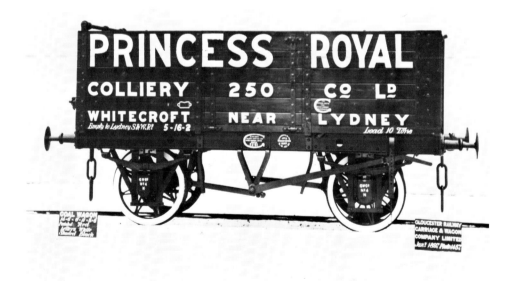

TUFTS JUNCTION

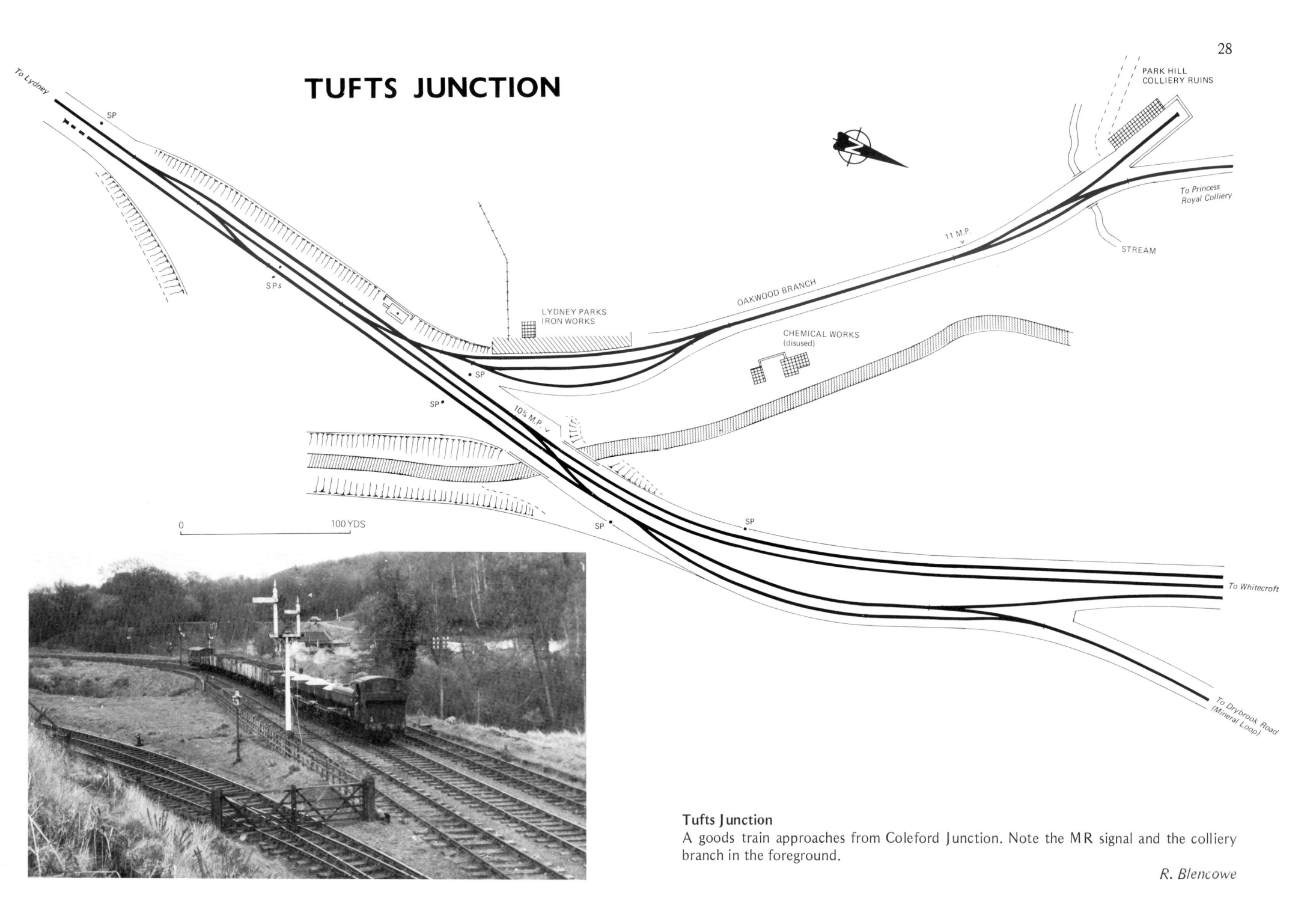

To Lydney

SP

SPs

SP

SP

SP

10¾ M.P.

0   100 YDS

LYDNEY PARKS
IRON WORKS

CHEMICAL WORKS
(disused)

OAKWOOD BRANCH

11 M.P.

PARK HILL
COLLIERY RUINS

To Princess
Royal Colliery

STREAM

To Whitecroft

To Drybrook Road
(Mineral Loop)

SP

SP

Tufts Junction
A goods train approaches from Coleford Junction. Note the MR signal and the colliery branch in the foreground.

R. Blencowe

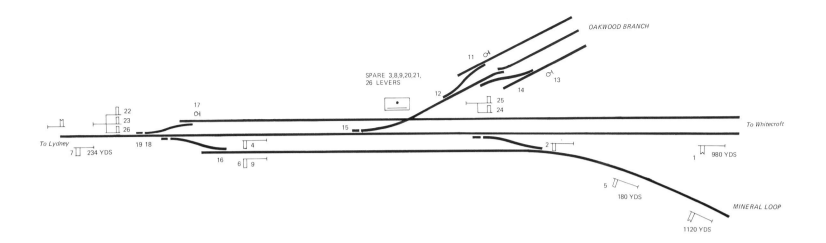

Tufts Junction

A train from Coleford Junction heads south, past the junction, in 1965. At this time, the MR signals still remained in use.

R. Blencowe

A wagon of the Gloucester Railway Carriage & Wagon Co. Ltd., which was built in December 1893. The livery is red, with white lettering, shaded black. It has black ironwork.

OPC Collection

Whitecroft

A view from the level crossing.

Lens of Sutton

WHITECROFT

Opened: 23rd September 1875
Closed: 6th July 1929 (to passenger); 2nd October 1967 (to freight)
Date of survey: 1920
Date of signalling plan: 1960

Whitecroft was opened in 1875 for the commencement of the S&W passenger service. It served a village in the Lyd Valley and, on opening, it had a single platform on the 'up' side, with the usual S&W wooden station building. A level crossing, which gave access to the platform, was at the northern end.

In 1897, a second platform was added and the line was doubled to Parkend. A siding looped behind this platform to serve the small wooden goods shed, and a signal box was opened next to the crossing.

A siding ran from Tufts Junction to serve the Patent Fuel Works until its closure in 1925. The station closed to passengers in 1929 and in November 1930, the main line was singled north of the station and the signal box was replaced by an eight lever ground frame, and in 1941, a new siding, off the goods shed road, was provided for Roads Construction Ltd. All the sidings and the 'down' main line were removed in 1964 with the exception of the goods shed siding, which lasted until 1967, leaving a single running line through the site. This has been out of use since 1976, although, at the time of writing, maintenance is continuing.

Whitecroft

A stone train from Whitecliff Quarry passes the station. Note the ground frame hut on the left.

R. Blencowe

WHITECROFT

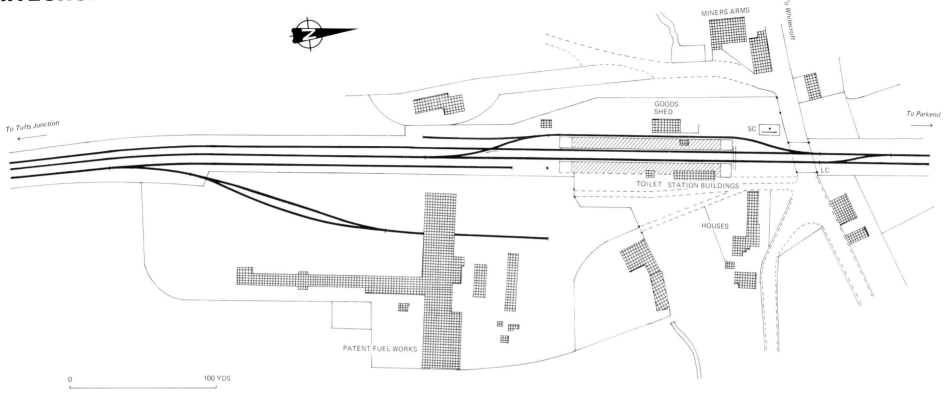

MINERS ARMS

To Whitecroft

To Parkend

GOODS
SHED

SC

To Tufts Junction

TOILET   STATION BUILDINGS

LC

HOUSES

PATENT FUEL WORKS

0   100 YDS

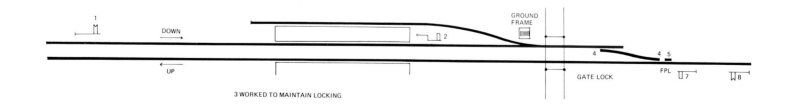

1

GROUND
FRAME

DOWN   2

4   4   5

UP   GATE LOCK   FPL   7   8

3 WORKED TO MAINTAIN LOCKING

31

Whitecroft
The station, looking south, circa 1960.

Lens of Sutton

Whitecroft
The station, circa 1910, showing the wooden platform shelter on the left.

Lens of Sutton

Whitecroft
A view, facing north, on the original S & W platform.

Lens of Sutton

Whitecroft
A view of the station, as seen on 23rd June 1962.

S. Clarkson

PARKEND

Opened: 23rd September 1875 (to passengers)
Closed: 6th July 1929 (to passengers); Mineral trains continued until 1976
Date of survey: (a) 1880 (b) 1920
Date of signalling plan: July 1962

The importance of Parkend preceded the railway, for it was an important crossroads in the tramway network from the early 1800s until the opening of the S & W, as a railway, in 1868. Even then the tramways remained in use well into the 1880s, serving areas not reached by the railway.

The first plan shows the situation in 1880, with the railway and tramways existing side by side, and the station which had opened in 1875. The large works is Parkend Iron & Tin Plate Works, which had actually ceased production in 1877, but the plan does show how the tramways served the Works when it was in use. The complexity of lines is astonishing, and all were worked by horses, including those running over the famous 'covered way', which crossed the S&W line to serve the ironworks. The various interchange points between the railway and the tramway are interesting, as these can only have been short-lived. Most of the industrial buildings were removed in 1890, although the large engine house remains. The 'covered way' was demolished in 1898 and little sign of it now remains.

The second plan shows the area in 1920 and, in fact, the railway layout has not changed a great deal, although the area itself has. The goods shed, a wooden structure, was built in the 1890s by the S&W to replace an earlier one which was situated 500 yards south of the station to the west of the main line. Parkend was an important station, having two platforms, a footbridge and a large GWR-type wooden signal box. It closed in 1929 along with the other S&W stations north of Lydney and it was the passenger junction for Coleford.

The main line south of the station was singled in 1930, but little else changed until the 1960s. The signal box closed on 2nd October 1967 following closure of the line north of Parkend. Ballast from Whitecliff Quarry continued to be loaded at Parkend Marsh Sidings, with a little coal, until traffic ceased in 1976. Until 1978, the station was also the temporary base for the Dean Forest Railway Society. The line to Parkend remains in place, although unused, and the society hope to purchase it from British Rail.

Parkend
A view looking down on to the station from the ironworks' tips, circa 1910, with GWR and MR vans seen on the siding, and a train of GWR coaches in the platform.

Lens of Sutton

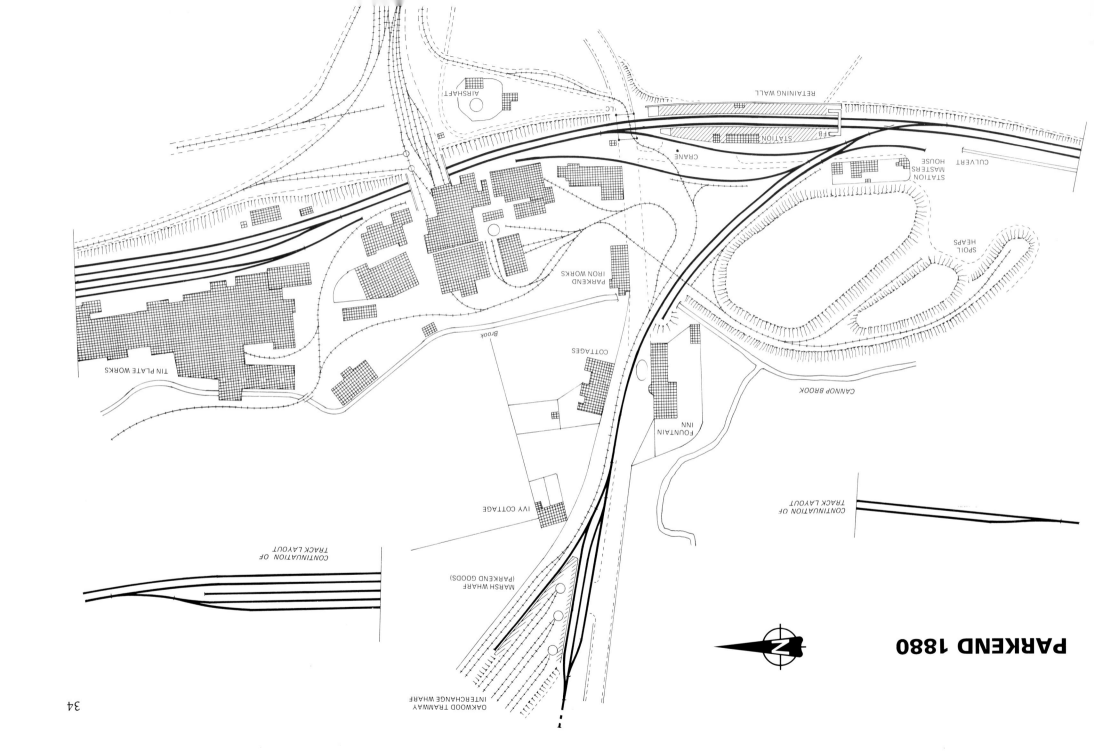

PARKEND 1880

N

RETAINING WALL

AIRSHAFT

LC

STATION

FB

CRANE

CULVERT

STATION MASTERS HOUSE

SPOIL HEAPS

CANNOP BROOK

PARKEND IRON WORKS

Brook

TIN PLATE WORKS

COTTAGES

FOUNTAIN INN

IVY COTTAGE

CONTINUATION OF TRACK LAYOUT

CONTINUATION OF TRACK LAYOUT

MARSH WHARF
(PARKEND GOODS)

CONTINUATION OF TRACK LAYOUT

OAKWOOD TRAMWAY
INTERCHANGE WHARF

PARKEND 1920

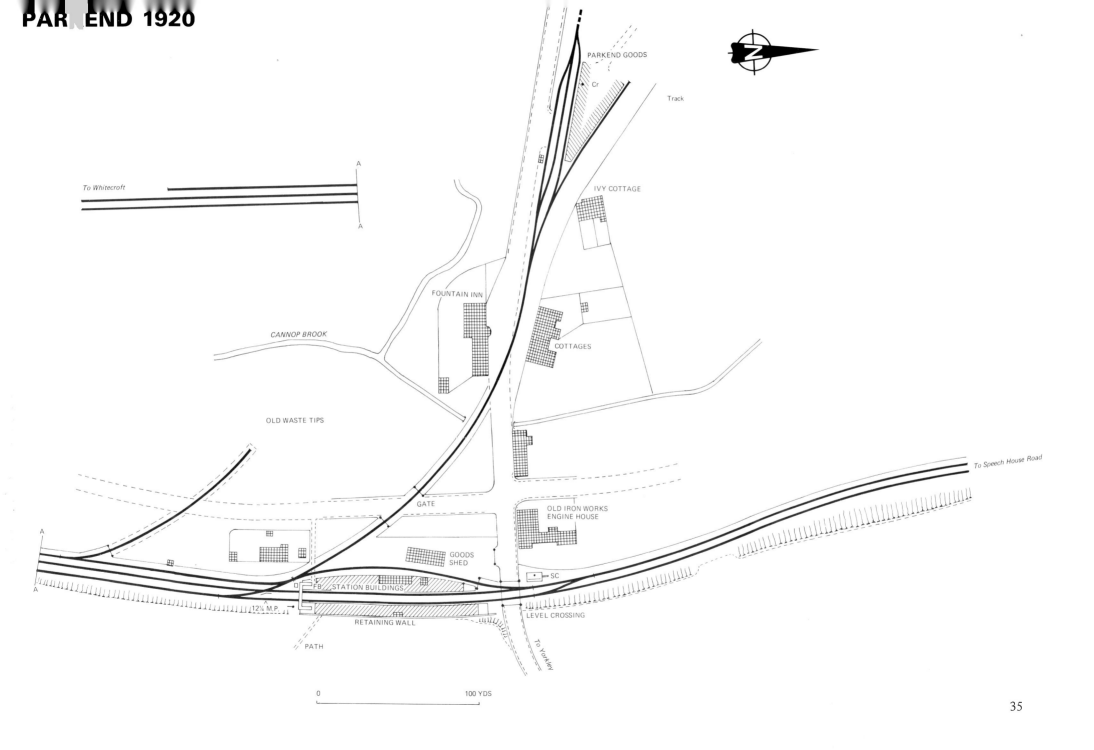

To Whitecroft

PARKEND GOODS

Cr

Track

IVY COTTAGE

FOUNTAIN INN

CANNOP BROOK

COTTAGES

OLD WASTE TIPS

To Speech House Road

GATE

OLD IRON WORKS
ENGINE HOUSE

GOODS
SHED

SC

FB STATION BUILDINGS

12¼ M.P.

RETAINING WALL

LEVEL CROSSING

PATH

To Yorkley

0   100 YDS

35

Parkend

The station, circa 1910.

Lens of Sutton

Parkend

A view looking north across the station, in 1960, showing the station master's house.

Lens of Sutton

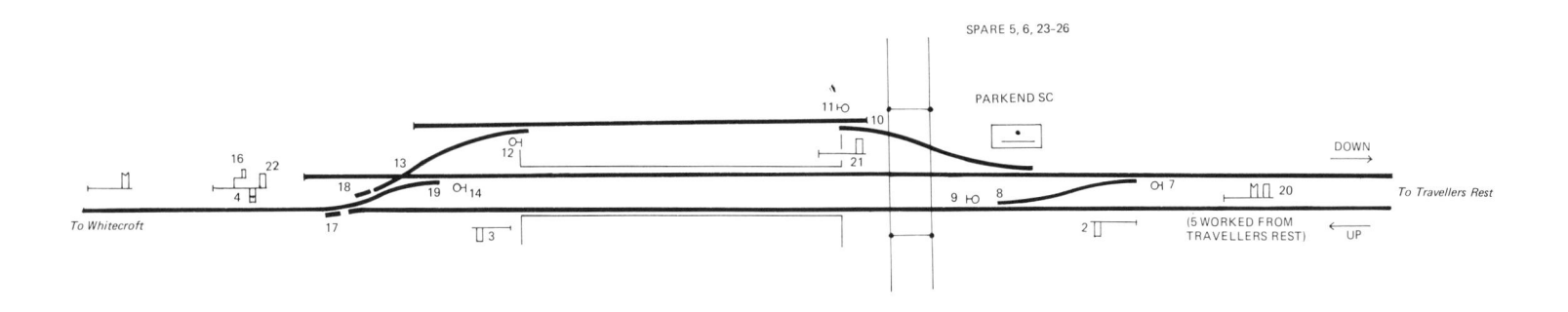

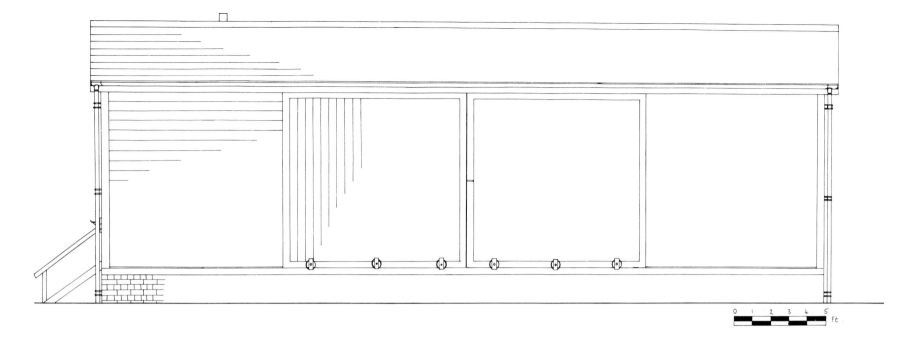

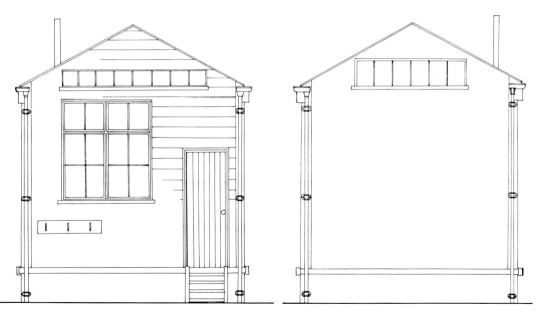

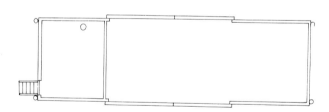

PARKEND GOODS SHED

The goods shed at Parkend is, for it still survives, of the standard S&W design erected, with minor differences, at most stations on the system. Built of wood, with sliding doors on both sides and a loading platform within, it stood beside the loop siding. An office, which houses a stove, is built into one end. The roof is slated and the walls have horizontal planks. In S&W days, the main building was of a light stone colour, with chocolate brown framing, and this changed little after the take-over in 1894. By 1946, the building was painted in a dark colour, all over; probably brown.

Parkend
Pannier tank No. 4689 takes water at the station in August 1965.

R. Blencowe

Parkend
A mixed goods train runs into the station behind No. 4614, in 1964.

S. Clarkson

Parkend
A 'Dean Goods' 0-6-0 locomotive, unusual in the Forest, on a permanent way train, at Parkend, on 21st September 1947. Note the gas lamp and MR signal.

P. Copeland

Parkend
A southbound train takes the token for the single line section, south of Parkend, in 1967.

R. Blencowe

Parkend

No. 4614 takes water at Parkend on 31st July 1964, beneath the S & W footbridge.
S. Clarkson

Parkend

A Gloucestershire Railway Society train pictured at Parkend in June 1962.
S. Clarkson

COLEFORD JUNCTION AND TRAVELLERS REST

Opened: 9th September 1875
Closed: 2nd October 1967 (last traffic 11th August 1967)
Date of survey: 1910
Date of signalling plan: 1960

These two locations really form part of the same layout as they were the marshalling sidings where the Coleford branch diverged from the main line. The junction faced Cinderford, a factor dictated by the lay of the land, and many mineral trains reached Lydney by first running north and then down the mineral loop. A triangle was proposed at the junction, but was never built. Two signal boxes controlled the loops and the junction; Travellers Rest, in the south, named after a nearby public house, and Coleford Junction in the north. At Travellers Rest, on the 'down' side, a siding served a stone saw-mill, until 1911, and on the 'up' side a short branch diverged to Parkend Royal Colliery. This siding was removed in 1940. Another stone sawmill was once adjacent to this until its closure in 1932.

Coleford Junction signal box was originally a wooden-gabled building, but this was replaced by a small GWR box in 1925, on the same site. This remained in use up to the closure of the line, in 1967, the lines having survived, until then, for stone traffic from Whitecliff Quarry.

COLEFORD JUNCTION

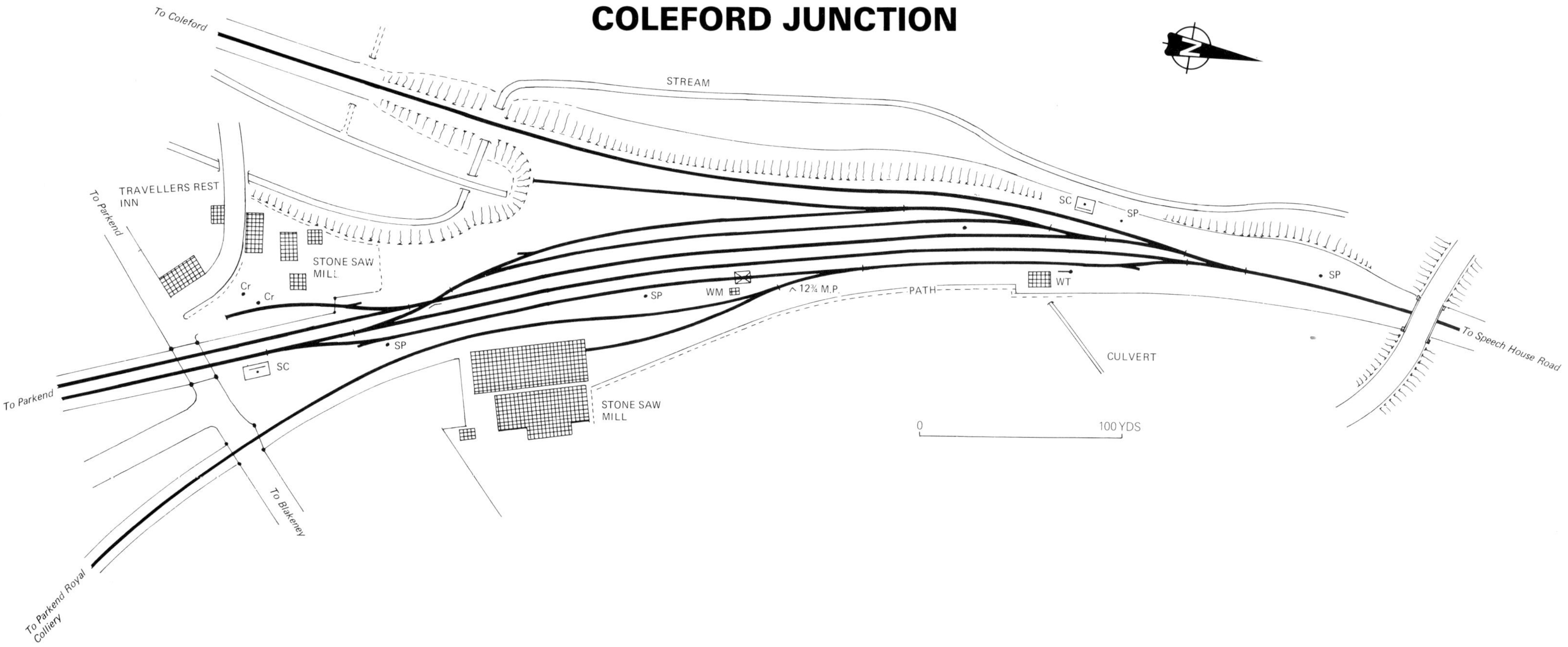

SPARE 2 — 4
SPACE 7, 16–19, 14, 15

22 LEVERS

TRAVELLERS REST
SC

23 LEVERS
SPARE 1, 7 – 9, 23

COLEFORD
JUNCTION
SC

UP GOODS LOOP

UP

DOWN

DOWN SIDINGS

To Coleford
(One Loco in steam)

To Speech House Road

STONE SAW MILL

CULVERT

100 YDS

0

PATH

WT

SP

12% M.P

WM

SP

SP

SP

SC

SC

STREAM

STONE SAW MILL

SP

SC SC

Cr.
Cr.
Cr.
STONE SAW MILL

TRAVELLERS REST
INN

To Parkend

To Parkend Royal Colliery

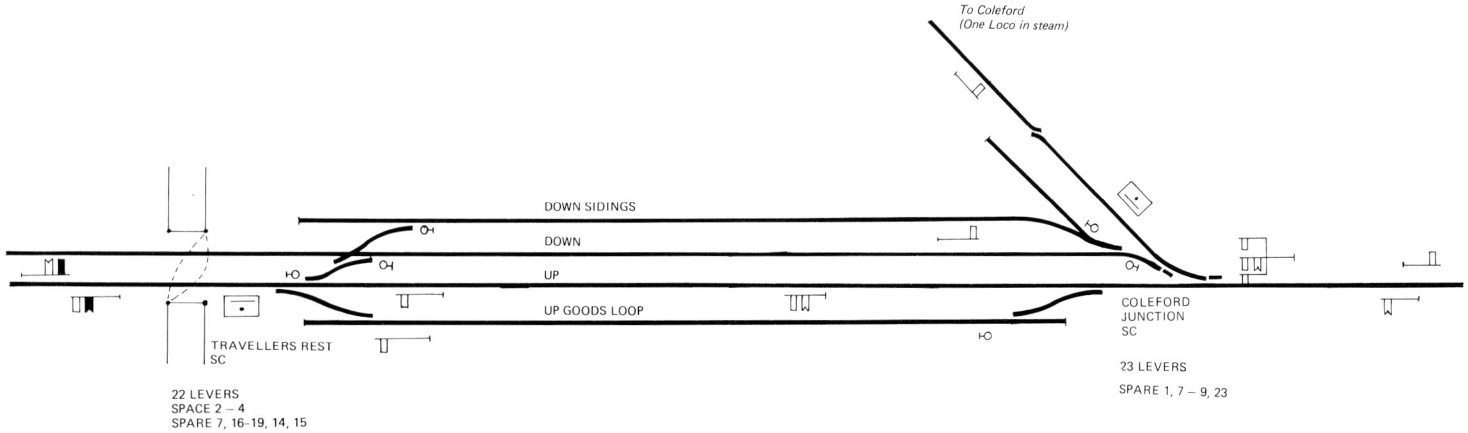

To Blakeney

To Parkend

To Coleford

Travellers Rest
A view looking south, towards Travellers Rest Crossing, in 1965.

R. Blencowe

Travellers Rest
Stone from Whitecliff Quarry passes the crossing in 1965, hiding the signal box.

R. Blencowe

Travellers Rest
A northbound train has just passed the signal box. The line to Parkend Royal Colliery is on the right.

P. Copeland

Travellers Rest
The crossing and signal box.

S. Clarkson

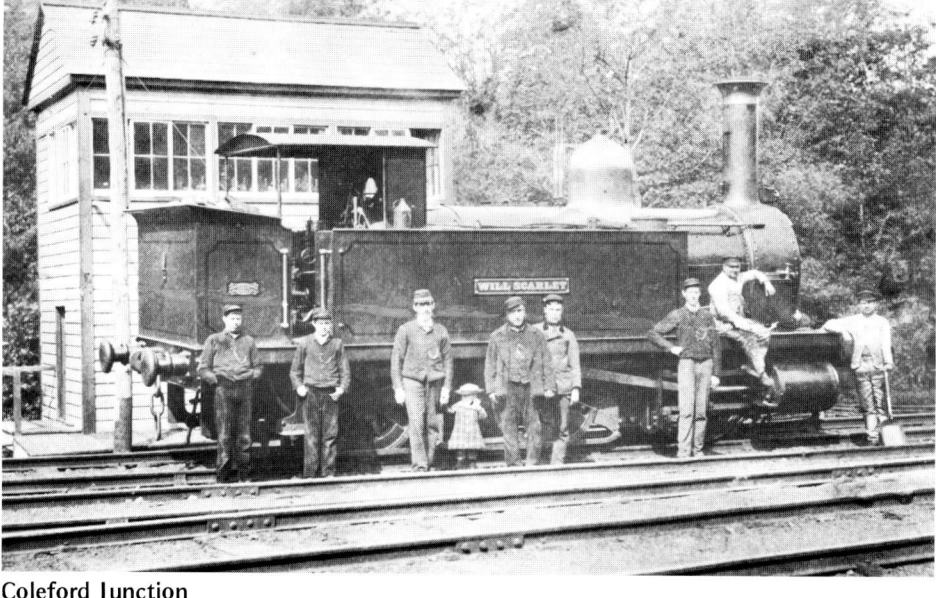

Coleford Junction

Severn & Wye locomotive *Will Scarlet* poses in front of the original signal box at Coleford Junction, circa 1890. Note the light track used by the S & W, with its flat-bottomed rail.

DFRS

Coleford Junction

A view looking north from the junction, with the hut for the line inspection trolleys seen on the left.

R. Blencowe

Coleford Junction

No. 4698 brings a short freight on to the loop siding in August 1965.

R. Blencowe

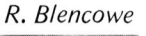

Coleford Junction

A view of the later signal box, looking south.

R. Blencowe

Coleford Junction
As a comparison, this is *Will Scarlet* in 1911, after being rebuilt by the GWR. Little of the original engine remains above the footplate other than the nameplates. In fact, the GWR, when rebuilding, usually changed the nameplates.

HMRS

Coleford Junction
A view, from the road bridge, looking towards the junction.

S. Clarkson

Coleford Junction
The GWR signal box.

S. Clarkson

BICSLADE TRAMWAY WHARF

Opened: circa 1868
Closed: Last used 1946
Date of survey: 1910

  Bicslade Wharf was a simple interchange point between the railway and the Bicslade Tramway, which ran to Bixhead Quarries which were deep in the Forest. The stone was transferred into the railway wagons at the wharf, where there were a number of cranes. The tramway, a relic of the original S&W line, remained in use until 1946, and was the last survivor of this old method of transport. The siding at the wharf remained in place, out of use, until the closure of the line on 12th August 1963.

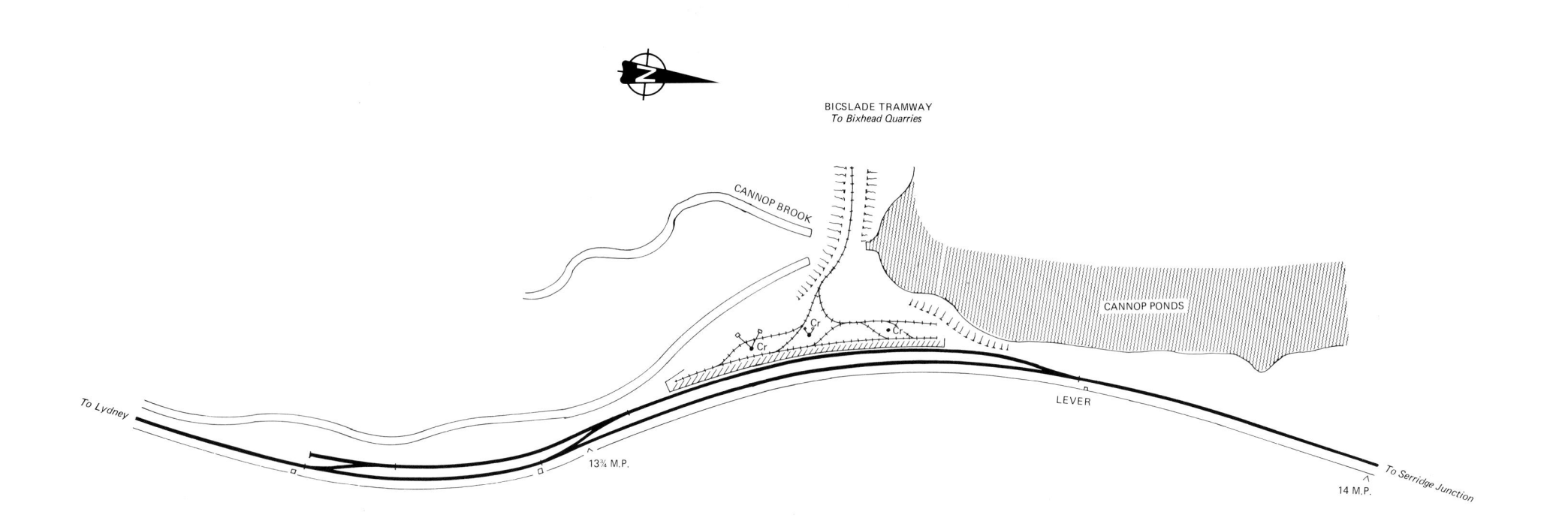

Speech House Road
A train for Lydney stands in the platform, circa 1915, behind a GWR 0-6-0 saddle tank, of the 2021 class.

Lens of Sutton

SPEECH HOUSE ROAD AND THE WIMBERRY BRANCH

Opened: 23rd September 1875 (station)
Closed: 6th July 1929
Date of survey: 1900
Date of signalling plan: 1955

Speech House Road Station was situated just south of the level crossing by which the famous road of the same name crossed the S & W line. The station, and road, were named after the Forest Parliament Building, situated a couple of miles from the station in the heart of the Forest. The station had one platform, with the usual wooden station building, and a GWR signal box stood opposite. Beyond the crossing was a well-built brick house for the station master. A siding served a small wooden goods shed and another served a wharf on which terminated the Howlers Slade Tramway. A stone sawmill also made use of the wharf.

The junction of the Wimberry branch was north of the station. This line was important in the early years, being the northern terminus of the original broad gauge line of 1868. The branch terminated at Hopewell Sidings, from which a tramway ran to Wimberry Colliery. Another connection from the main line ran to Speech House Colliery.

This was the situation at the time of the survey in 1910, but two years later, considerable changes took place, as shown on the second plan, which is not drawn to scale. In 1912, the branch was extended, alongside the main line, to the station, where a new junction was put in north of the level crossing. A new pit, Cannop Colliery, was opened on the branch, and this pit was served by new sidings, while in 1914, the old branch to Speech House Colliery, which had closed in 1906, was removed. In 1917, a new siding was laid at the station to serve a new wood distillation plant.

The station closed in 1929, and in 1946, traffic ceased on the branch beyond Cannop Colliery, which remained open until 1960. All traffic ceased north of Speech House Road on 21st November 1960.

Speech House Road
A view looking north, in 1948, from a passing train.

P. Copeland

To Parkend

To Coleford

STATION
MASTERS
HOUSE

STONE SAW MILLS

Cr
Cr Cr
•Cr •Cr •Cr

GS
SC
•Cr

SB

14¾ M.P.

To Cinderford

To Serridge Junction

0   100 YDS

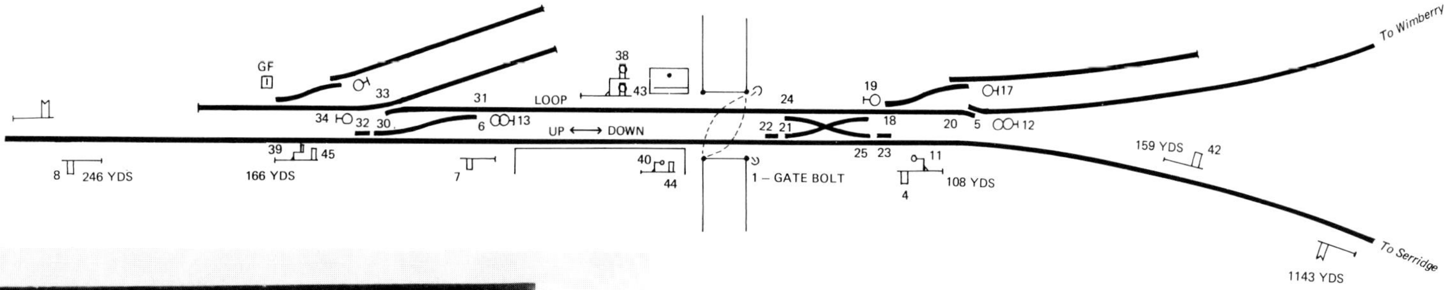

To Wimberry

GF

38
43

24

19
17

33

31   LOOP

34 32 30

6 13

UP ← → DOWN

22 21

18

20 5 12

39 45

7

40
44

1 – GATE BOLT

25 23

11
4

108 YDS

159 YDS 42

8 246 YDS

166 YDS

To Serridge

1143 YDS

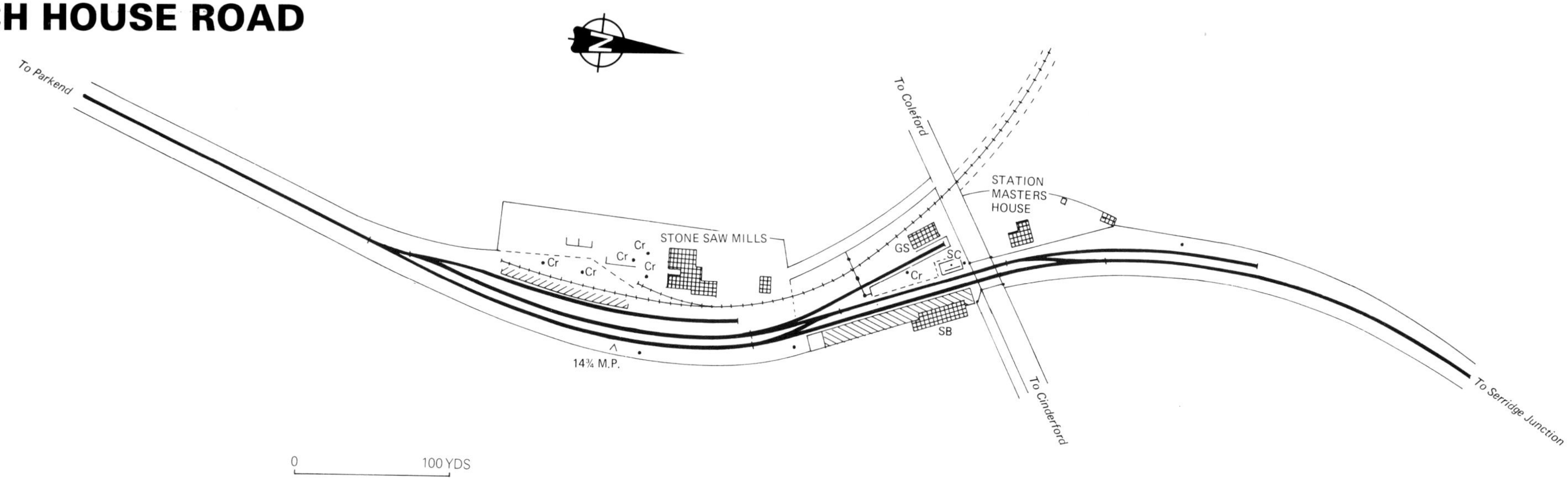

A wagon of the Gloucester Railway Carriage & Wagon Co. Ltd., which was built in March 1893. The livery is black, and it is lettered in white. Note the unusual use of metal framing.

OPC Collection

Speech House Road
The large GWR signal box, seen after closure, with the station master's house beyond.
Lens of Sutton

Speech House Road
The last train, seen south of the station, behind No. 1664, in June 1964.
R. Blencowe

Speech House Road
A view looking south, after closure of the station.
Lens of Sutton

Speech House Road
The station, in May 1961, still virtually intact.
S. Clarkson

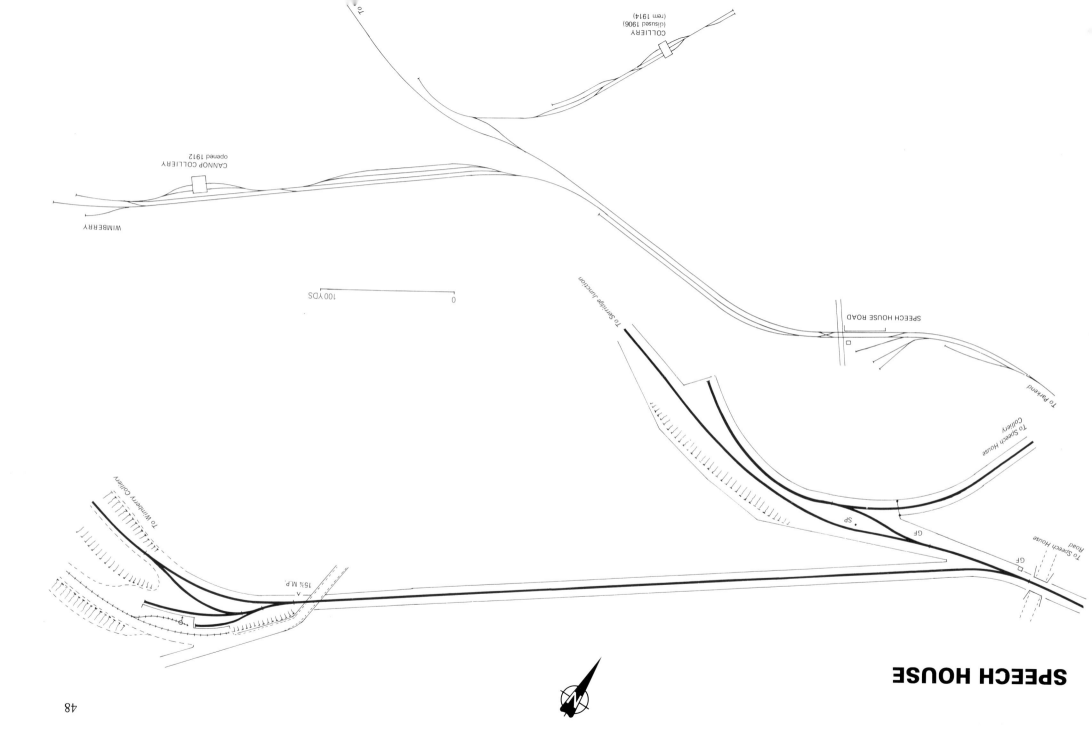

SPEECH HOUSE

COLLIERY
(disused 1906)
(rem 1914)

CANNOP COLLIERY
opened 1912

WIMBERRY

To

100 YDS

To Serridge Junction

SPEECH HOUSE ROAD

To Parkend

To Speech House
Colliery

To Wimberry Colliery

To Speech House

15% M.P.

SP

GF

To Speech House
Road

GF

SERRIDGE JUNCTION

Opened: 19th April 1869
Closed: 21st November 1960
Date of survey: 1920

The Lydbrook line diverged from the S&W main line at Serridge Junction and the junction faced Cinderford. Mineral trains ran south, via the mineral loop, from Drybrook Road. The junction was controlled from a small wooden signal box, which had been moved from Lydney Town in 1896. The main line was single, but there were two loops on the branch, with a water-tower and an inspection trolley shed. Just south of the junction, Crown Siding, put in during 1903, left the main line. It was used for loading Crown Timber and was out of use by 1953.

In 1878, a platform was provided north of the junction for the keeper of Serridge Lodge, but this was removed about a year later.

Serridge Junction
A northbound train of empties approaches the junction in 1948, with the Lydbrook line on the left.

P. Copeland

Serridge Junction
A retaining arch and wall between Serridge Junction and Drybrook Road, built when the Trafalgar Colliery tip threatened the line.

S. Clarkson

Serridge Junction
No. 2043 comes off the branch with a coal train from Mierystock.

P. Copeland

SERRIDGE JUNCTION

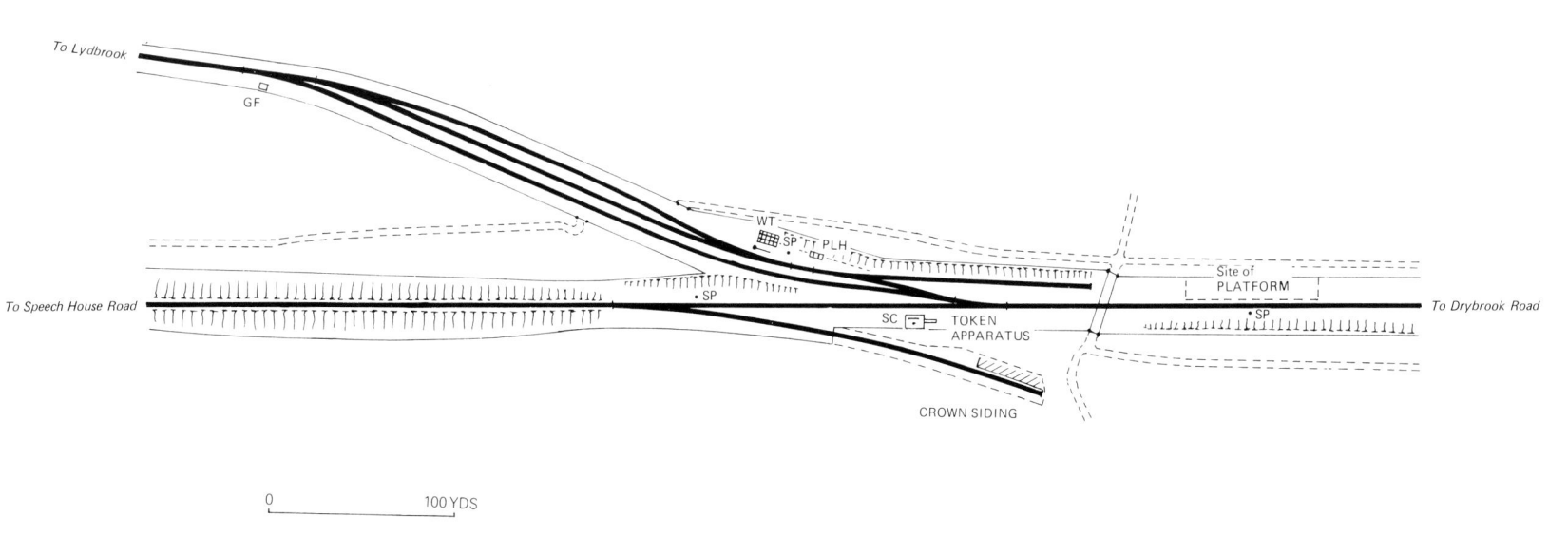

To Lydbrook

GF

To Speech House Road

WT

SP PLH

SP

SC TOKEN APPARATUS

Site of PLATFORM

SP

To Drybrook Road

CROWN SIDING

0   100 YDS

TRAFALGAR COLLIERY AND DRYBROOK ROAD

Opened: 23rd September 1876 (Drybrook Road)
Closed: 6th July 1929 (Drybrook Road)
Date of survey: 1920 (Drybrook Road)
                     1890 (Trafalgar Colliery)

Trafalgar Colliery lay to the north of the main line near Drybrook Road Station, and the two will be considered together. Drybrook Road was a small one platform station, with a wooden station building and goods shed next to a level crossing. Beyond this was the station master's house. The importance of the station lay in the fact that it was the northern junction of the mineral loop line. Both lines had passing loops, becoming single before the junction.

The railway connection to the colliery replaced the Trafalgar Tramway, although this remained in place for some years. The name of the pit reflected the period in which it

opened, about 1815. A loop, off the running line, served the colliery sidings, and was worked from a signal box. In 1892, this arrangement was superseded, when a new signal box was opened at Drybrook Road and the siding to the colliery was extended to join the main line at the station. It formed a connection with the mineral loop, via a double slip; an unusual arrangement that allowed through running to take place. The 15 chain siding served the colliery screens and traffic declined in the 1920s, culminating in the closure of the signal box on 17th May 1927 when it became a ground frame. The station closed in 1929 and the freight service was withdrawn in 1949. The track was severed in 1950 and the mineral loop, officially, remained open until 1953.

The station building at Drybrook Road is interesting in that it was moved to the station in 1900 from Cinderford (old) Station and can now be seen at Norchard Railway Centre. It is the only preserved S & W station building.

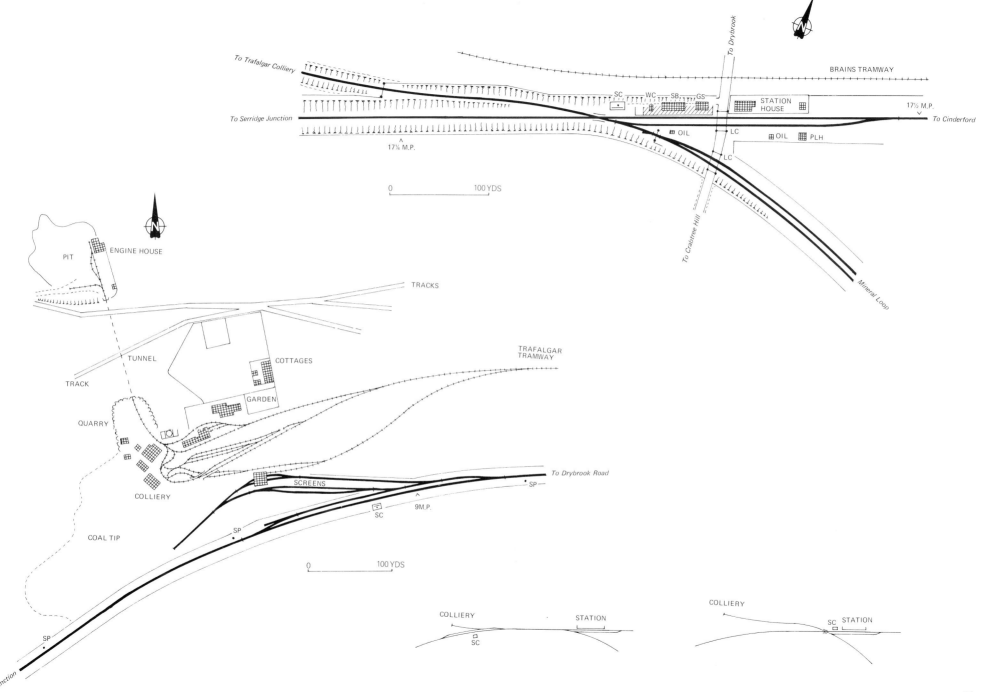

To Trafalgar Colliery

To Serridge Junction

BRAINS TRAMWAY

To Drybrook

SC WC SB GS

STATION HOUSE

17½ M.P.

To Cinderford

17¼ M.P.

OIL LC

OIL PLH

LC

To Crabtree Hill

Mineral Loop

0 100 YDS

PIT ENGINE HOUSE

TRACKS

TUNNEL

TRACK

COTTAGES

GARDEN

QUARRY

TRAFALGAR TRAMWAY

COLLIERY

To Drybrook Road

SP

SCREENS

SP

SC 9 M.P.

COAL TIP

SP

SP

0 100 YDS

To Serridge Junction

COLLIERY STATION

SC

COLLIERY STATION

SC

Drybrook Road
A view looking west, with the station master's house on the right.

P. Copeland

Drybrook Road
The overgrown mineral loop line, as seen in 1947. There was a passing loop beyond the signal.

P. Copeland

Drybrook Road
A view looking towards the station from the junction, showing the mineral loop.

P. Copeland

Drybrook Road
A view looking west from the junction, with the connection to Trafalgar Colliery on the right of the main line.

P. Copeland

CINDERFORD (OLD) STATION

Opened: 5th August 1878
Closed: 2nd July 1900
Date of survey: 1920

When the S&W began its passenger service to Cinderford in 1875, a temporary wooden platform was built on the site of the junction. The Crump Meadow Colliery branch was not then built. Known as Bilson Platform, it sufficed for three years while the site for a permanent station was decided upon. For a plan of the area during this period, please refer to Bilson Junction.

The new station was finally opened, in 1878, on the northern spur of the junctions with the GWR Churchway mineral branch. There was a single platform with a wooden station building, the approach from Cinderford being along a narrow and, no doubt, muddy path. Facilities were minimal and trains reversed here before continuing their journeys to terminate at Lydney or Lydbrook Junction. Amid growing complaints, the station lasted until 1900, when the new joint committee built a new station close to Cinderford itself. As mentioned earlier, the station building can now be seen at Norchard.

Although the plan shows the site in 1920, little had changed, and the layout was the same as it had been, with the exception of run-round facilities.

The new extension of 1900 can be clearly seen running on an embankment to cross the GWR lines. The S&W junctions lasted until line closure on 9th December 1951. The site has now returned to nature, with little sign of the railway remaining.

For further plans of this area, including Cinderford Junction, see Bilson Junction.

Cinderford (Old) Station
Coal empties for Northern United Colliery pass the former junction with the S&W line. The line to the new Cinderford Station passed over the bridge.

B. J. Ashworth

CINDERFORD

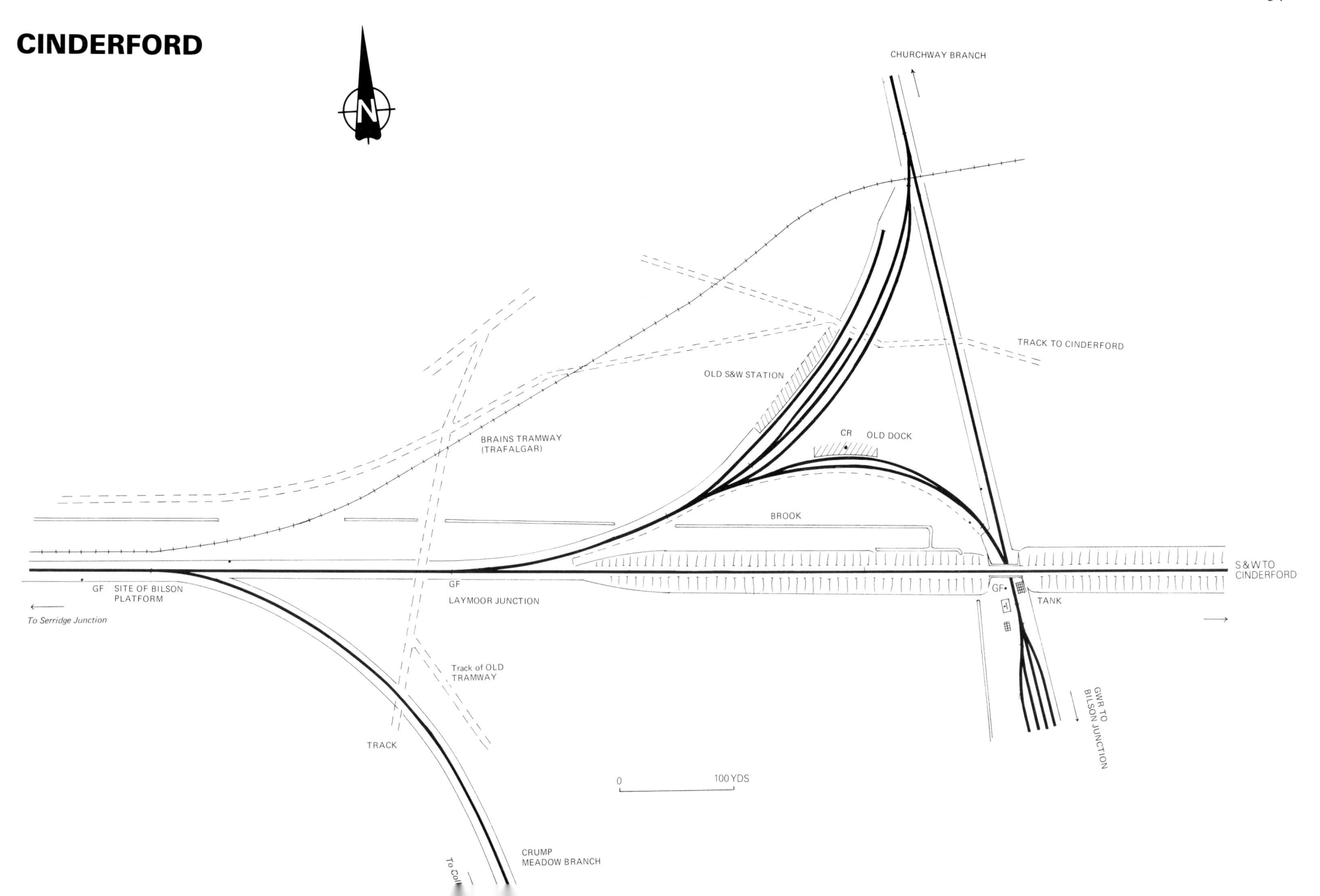

CHURCHWAY BRANCH

TRACK TO CINDERFORD

OLD S&W STATION

CR   OLD DOCK

BRAINS TRAMWAY
(TRAFALGAR)

BROOK

S&W TO
CINDERFORD

GF   SITE OF BILSON
PLATFORM

GF

GF

LAYMOOR JUNCTION

GF

TANK

To Serridge Junction

Track of OLD
TRAMWAY

GWR TO
BILSON JUNCTION

TRACK

0   100 YDS

CRUMP
MEADOW BRANCH

To Col

Cinderford (Old) Station
The scene in September 1965, with a train on the GWR Churchway line, which was part of the original GWR branch of 1854.

B. J. Ashworth

Cinderford (Old) Station
In 1946, the S&W lines were still in place, although scarcely used. The S&W terminus was at the top of the picture below the trees in this view facing due north.

P. Copeland

Cinderford Junction
A view looking towards Cinderford Station.

P. Copeland

Cinderford Junction
The junction as seen from the top of a signal post, in 1946.

P. Copeland

CINDERFORD

Opened: 2nd July 1900
Closed: 3rd November 1958 (to passengers); 11th August 1967 (to freight)
Date of survey: 1920

The GWR/MR Joint Committee lost no time in providing a new station for Cinderford, following their take-over of the Severn & Wye Railway in 1894. The new station opened in 1900, replacing the old S&W station and the line was carried from Laymoor Junction, on an embankment which crossed the GWR Churchway and Whimsey lines, before swinging south to the new station. The terminus was built by the GWR in their standard style of architecture, with a single platform, stone buildings and a wooden signal box. S&W line trains, by then comprising an 0-6-0 saddle tank with GWR four-wheeled coaches, began using it at once.

On 6th April 1908, GWR trains from Newnham began using the station, via the new loop line from Bilson Junction. This introduced Cinderford Junction, where the loop joined the S&W line. GWR trains reversed out of Cinderford before continuing north to Drybrook and Nailbridge, this service lasting until 1930. The trains were always auto trains and, at first, comprised a 517 class 0-4-2 tank with a 70ft. trailer.

The GWR service rapidly became more important and the S&W trains ceased on 6th July 1929, the GW trains running until 1958. The signal box closed in 1927, although the building remained for many years. The S&W line was removed in 1951 and, thereafter, the station looked like any GWR branch line terminus. It remained open for parcels until 3rd January 1966 and it closed, totally, in 1967. The site has now been cleared.

Cinderford
The station, circa 1910, with a train just arriving.

Lens of Sutton

Cinderford
A pannier tank is seen shunting, circa 1920. Note the Midland Railway brake van under the loading gauge.

Lens of Sutton

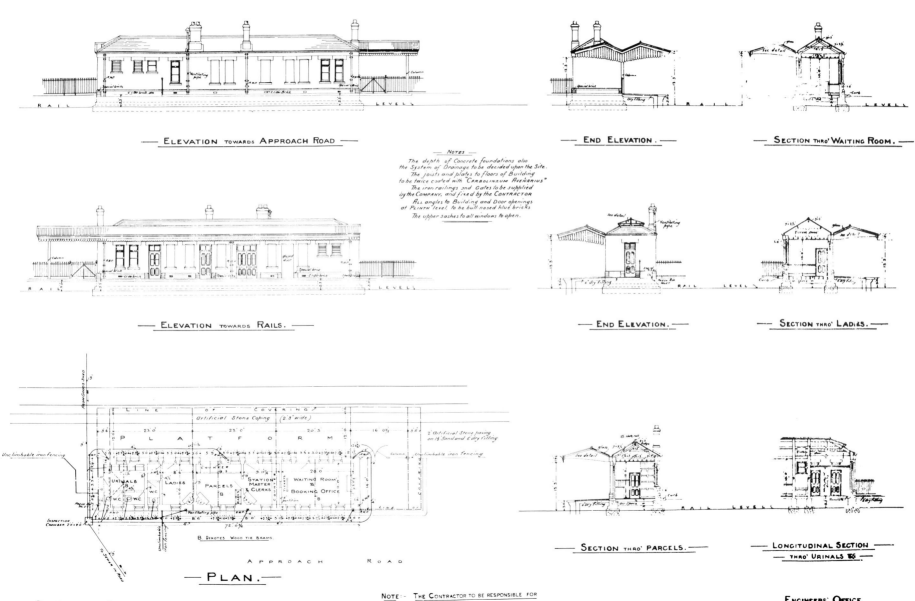

— ELEVATION TOWARDS APPROACH ROAD —

— END ELEVATION. —

— SECTION THRO' WAITING ROOM. —

NOTES

The depth of Concrete foundations also
the System of Drainage to be decided upon the Site.
The Joists and plates to floors of Building
to be twice coated with "Carbolineum Avenarius"
The iron railings and Gates to be supplied
by the Company, and fixed by the Contractor
All angles to Building and Door openings
at Plinth level, to be bull nosed blue bricks
The upper sashes to all windows to open.

— ELEVATION TOWARDS RAILS. —

— END ELEVATION. —

— SECTION THRO' LADIES. —

— SECTION THRO' PARCELS. —

— LONGITUDINAL SECTION THRO' URINALS &c —

— PLAN. —

— SCALE 8 FEET TO AN INCH —

NOTE :- THE CONTRACTOR TO BE RESPONSIBLE FOR
THE ACCURACY OF ALL LEADING DIMENSIONS

ENGINEERS' OFFICE
PADDINGTON

57

Note :- The Depth of the Concrete Foundations also the system of Drainage to be decided upon the Site.
The Floor joists and plates of Shed to be creosoted.
The Floor joists and plates of Office to be 2ce Coated with Carbolineum Avenarius.

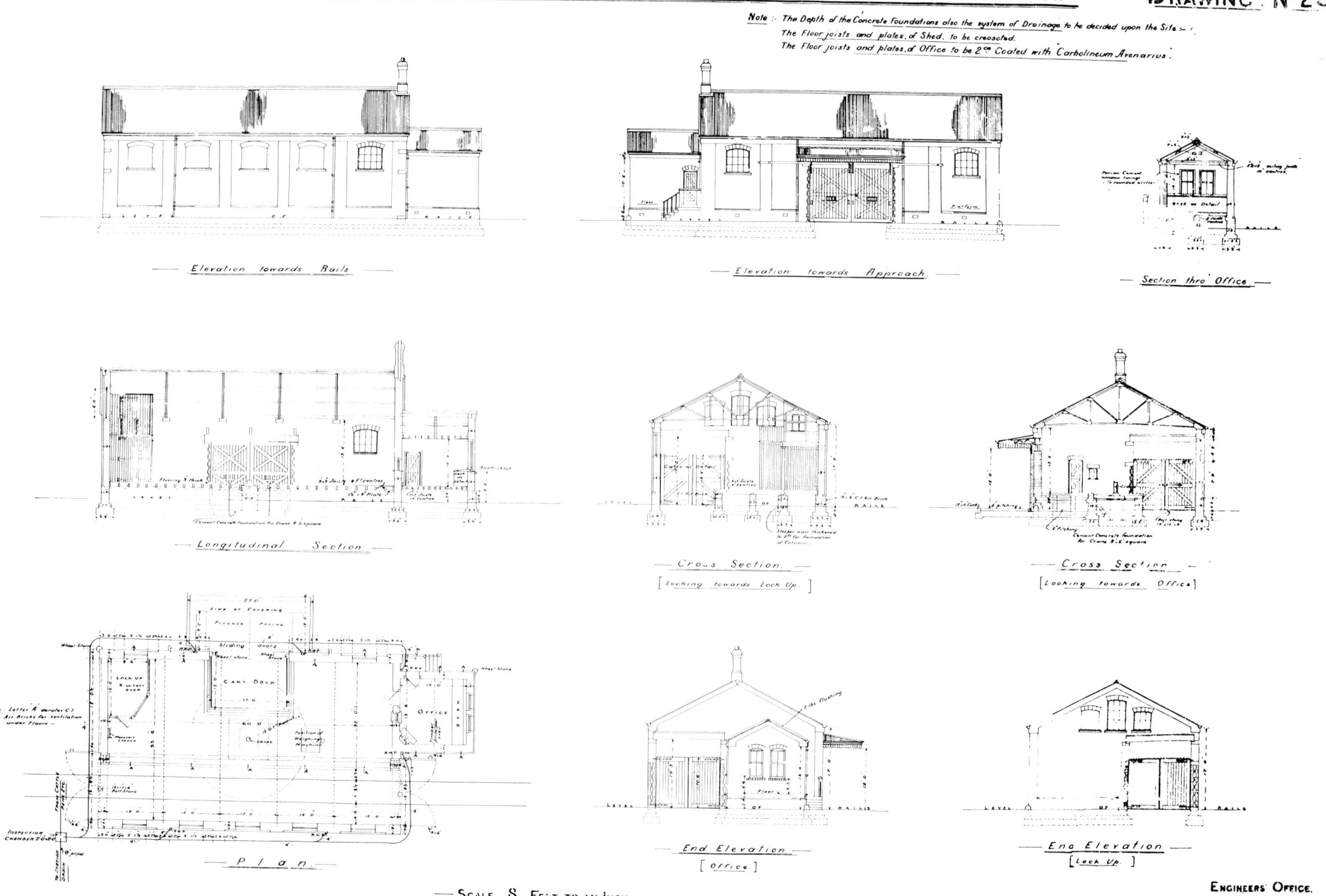

Elevation towards Rails

Elevation towards Approach.

Section thro' Office

Longitudinal Section

Cross Section.
[Looking towards Lock Up.]

Cross Section
[Looking towards Office.]

Note Letter A denotes C.I.
Air Bricks For ventilation
under Floors

Plan.

End Elevation
[Office]

End Elevation
[Lock Up.]

SCALE 8 FEET TO AN INCH

Engineers' Office.
Paddington

—— CINDERFORD EXTENSION RY ——

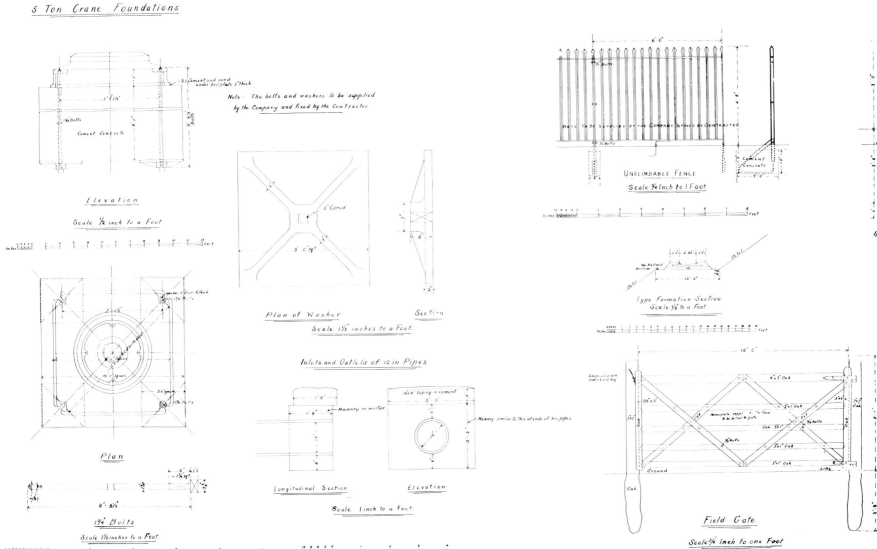

5 Ton Crane Foundations

Note: The bolts and washers to be supplied by the Company and fixed by the Contractor

Elevation

Scale ½ inch to a Foot

Plan of Washer

Section

Scale 1½ inches to a Foot

Plan

1¾ Bolts

Scale 1½ inches to a Foot

Inlets and Outlets of 12 in Pipes

Longitudinal Section

Elevation

Scale 1 inch to a Foot.

UNCLIMBABLE FENCE

Scale ¾ Inch to 1 Foot.

Type Formation Section

Scale ⅛ to a Foot

Field Gate

Scale ¾ Inch to one Foot

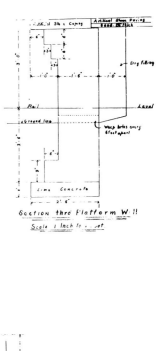

Section thro' Platform Wall

Scale 1 inch to a Foot

ENGINEER'S OFFICE,

PADDINGTON

59

Cinderford

No. 5408 heads a Newnham train on 10th September 1955. The canopy has been cut back on the road side of the station building.

H. Ballantyne

Cinderford

A pannier tank shunts the yard, after closure to passengers.

R. Blencowe

Cinderford

A view looking towards the buffer stops.

H. Ballantyne

Cinderford

The dismal scene in 1967, just before total closure.

Photomatic

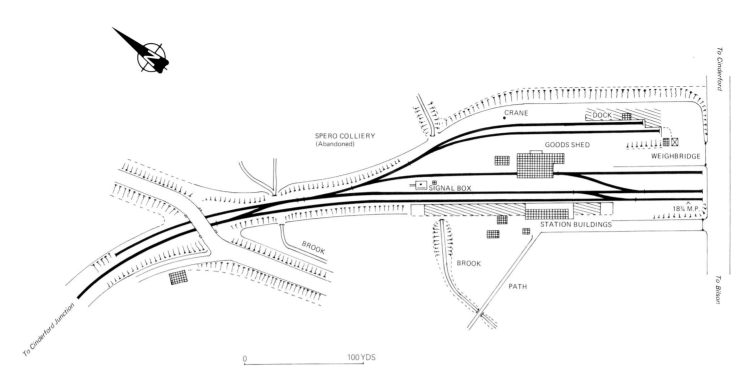

SPERO COLLIERY
(Abandoned)

CRANE

DOCK

GOODS SHED

WEIGHBRIDGE

SIGNAL BOX

STATION BUILDINGS

18¾ M.P.

BROOK

BROOK

PATH

To Cinderford

To Bilson

To Cinderford Junction

0   100 YDS

Cinderford
A train approaches the platform behind an 0-6-0 saddle tank, circa 1910.

Lens of Sutton

Cinderford
The station, just before closure, with 0-6-0PT No. 5408 on an auto train.

Lens of Sutton

SECTION 2

LYDNEY JUNCTION TO SHARPNESS (SEVERN BRIDGE RAILWAY AND SHARPNESS TO BERKELEY ROAD (MIDLAND RAILWAY)

This section was built in two parts. Both the Severn Bridge Railway and the Midland Railway's Sharpness line received their Acts in 1872, but the latter was the first to open. Running from Berkeley Road, on the Gloucester to Bristol main line, the branch ran to the newly-extended docks at Sharpness. This branch opened for freight on 2nd August 1875, and to passengers on 1st August 1876, with trains running to a temporary station at Sharpness.

The Severn Bridge line was a far greater undertaking and did not open, from Lydney Junction, until 17th October 1879, to a new station at Sharpness. The bridge itself was a great achievement, and, at that time, was second only to the Tay Bridge in length. It was 4,162 ft. long, with a thirteen arch stone approach viaduct on the Forest shore which spanned the GWR main line. The bridge had two 327 ft. spans and nineteen lesser ones plus a swing bridge of 197 ft. over the canal at Sharpness. The spans were of bowstring girders resting on cylindrical piers.

The lines gave the docks a great boost and traffic was run from the MR, GWR and S&W companies. In 1894, with the S&W take-over, the MR line passed to the S&W Joint Committee, the MR being responsible for maintaining this section.

Traffic on the line was heavy, and proposals had just been made to strengthen the bridge to allow heavier engines when, on 26th October 1960, a runaway barge collided with a pier, bringing down two spans. The decision was taken to demolish the bridge, and this was undertaken between 1968 and 1970. Little now remains to mark its site. The Sharpness to Berkeley Road passenger service lasted until 2nd November 1964, after which the line remained open only for freight traffic.

SEVERN BRIDGE STATION

Opened: 17th October 1879
Closed: 26th October 1960
Date of survey: 1920
Date of signalling plan: 1950

The Severn Bridge Railway was promoted by the S&W, the MR and the Gloucester & Berkeley Canal Co. The line ran from Lydney Junction to an end on junction, with the Midland Railway, at Sharpness.

The station at Severn Bridge was a small halt at the Forest end of the bridge, having two platforms with wooden shelters. Perched at the top of a high embankment, it had one siding serving a dock. The original tall wooden signal box stood on the Sharpness platform, but this was replaced, in 1911, by a MR cabin at the platform end. The station opened as 'Severn Bridge for Blakeney'.

After the damage to the Severn Bridge, in 1960, by a runaway barge, the station closed, rather abruptly, although the track remained until 1968.

Severn Bridge
The Severn Bridge from Sharpness, circa 1910, with the swing bridge at the nearer end.
Author's Collection

Severn Bridge
A train departs from Severn Bridge behind a 14XX 0-4-2T on 10th April 1948.
P. Copeland

Severn Bridge
The derelict station, circa 1965.

Lens of Sutton

Severn Bridge
A 'down' South Wales freight passes beneath the stone approach viaduct.

C. Maggs

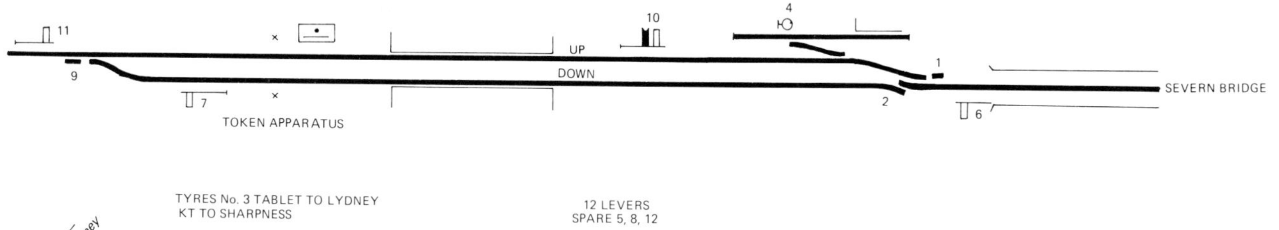

SEVERN BRIDGE

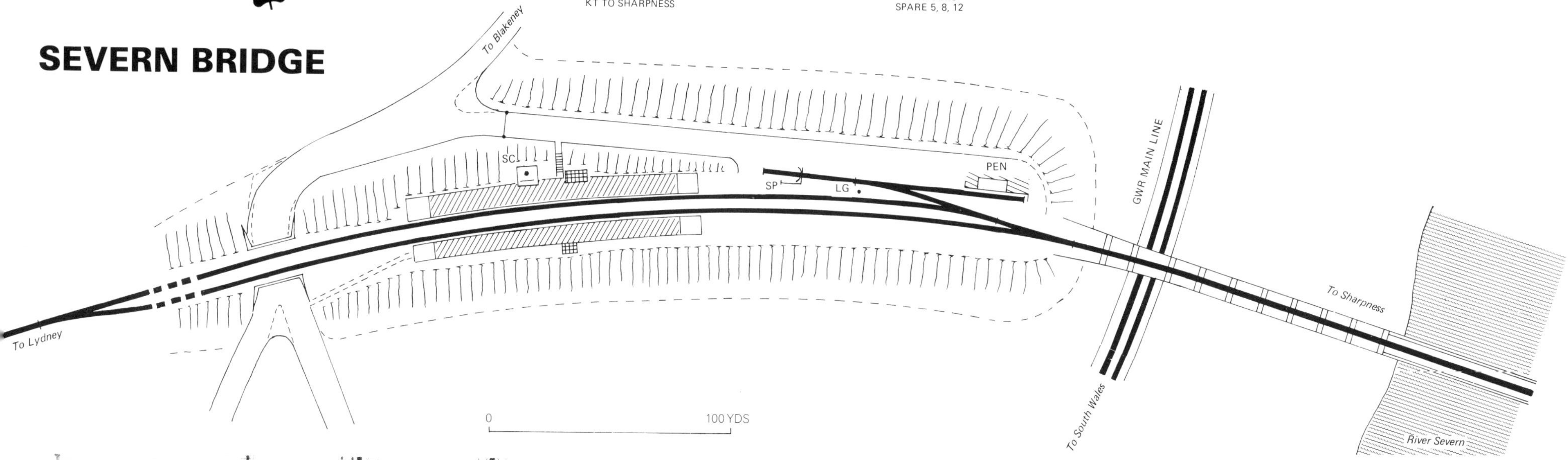

TYRES No. 3 TABLET TO LYDNEY
KT TO SHARPNESS

12 LEVERS
SPARE 5, 8, 12

TOKEN APPARATUS

UP

DOWN

SEVERN BRIDGE

To Blakeney

To Lydney

GWR MAIN LINE

To Sharpness

To South Wales

River Severn

SC · SP · LG · PEN

0   100 YDS

Severn Bridge
The view from the platform end, with a Berkeley Road train leaving.

HMRS

Severn Bridge
The station, after closure, but still intact.

C. Maggs

Severn Bridge
The Midland Railway signal box, in 1957.

S. Clarkson

Severn Bridge
The Severn Bridge from the Forest bank, in 1957.

S. Clarkson

Severn Bridge
Midland Railway fencing, a barrow and an LMS nameboard, at the station in 1957.

S. Clarkson

Severn Bridge
A view of the bridge and the station, circa 1900, showing the original SBR signal box which was replaced in 1912.

Author's Collection

Sharpness
A Severn & Wye and Severn Bridge Railway notice, circa 1880, at Sharpness photographed on 22nd October 1955.

F. W. Shuttleworth

SHARPNESS STATION AND DOCKS

Opened: 1st August 1876 (Original MR terminus)
 17th October 1879 (Second station)
Closed: 2nd November 1964 (to passengers)
Date of survey: 1932
Date of signalling plan: 1960

The docks at Sharpness preceded the railway, being established where the Gloucester & Berkeley Canal joined the River Severn, but not until the railway arrived, in 1875, did the port really flourish, taking a great deal of trade from Lydney. The first line to serve the docks was the Midland branch from Berkeley Road, which was opened on 2nd August 1875 to freight and on 1st August 1876 to a temporary passenger terminus at Sharpness. Extensive sidings served the docks, and these were worked by the dock company's own fleet of 0-4-0 saddle tanks, although the MR, S&W and GWR companies all had sidings.

The Severn Bridge line opened, from Lydney, on 17th October 1879, a new Sharpness Station being opened jointly with the MR, replacing the old terminus. S&W trains began running through to Berkeley Road and the MR gained running powers over the S&W, while Forest coal and goods was given access to a modern deep water port; a great advance on Lydney or Bullo Pill. Many passengers using Sharpness were dock workers and their families, although there were also three hotels in the vicinity.

Following the Grouping, the passenger service on the lines was largely in the hands of GWR stock, latterly an 0-6-0PT or 14XX 0-4-2T plus a 'B' Set. The damage to the Severn Bridge in 1960 led to the cutting back of the passenger trains to Sharpness, the service lasting only until 2nd November 1964. Rationalization had already begun and as early as 1931, the MR line was singled and the GWR station signal box, which had opened in 1903, closed in October 1957. The station was swept away during 1967.

The docks still generate enough goods traffic, especially grain, to keep the line open, although other items, such as atomic waste, have been transported. Shunting is now by diesel, but the rail link looks secure for many years to come.

Sharpness
The station, circa 1903/4. The GWR signal box was new in 1903 and the box which it replaced is just visible beyond the barrow crossing.

Lens of Sutton

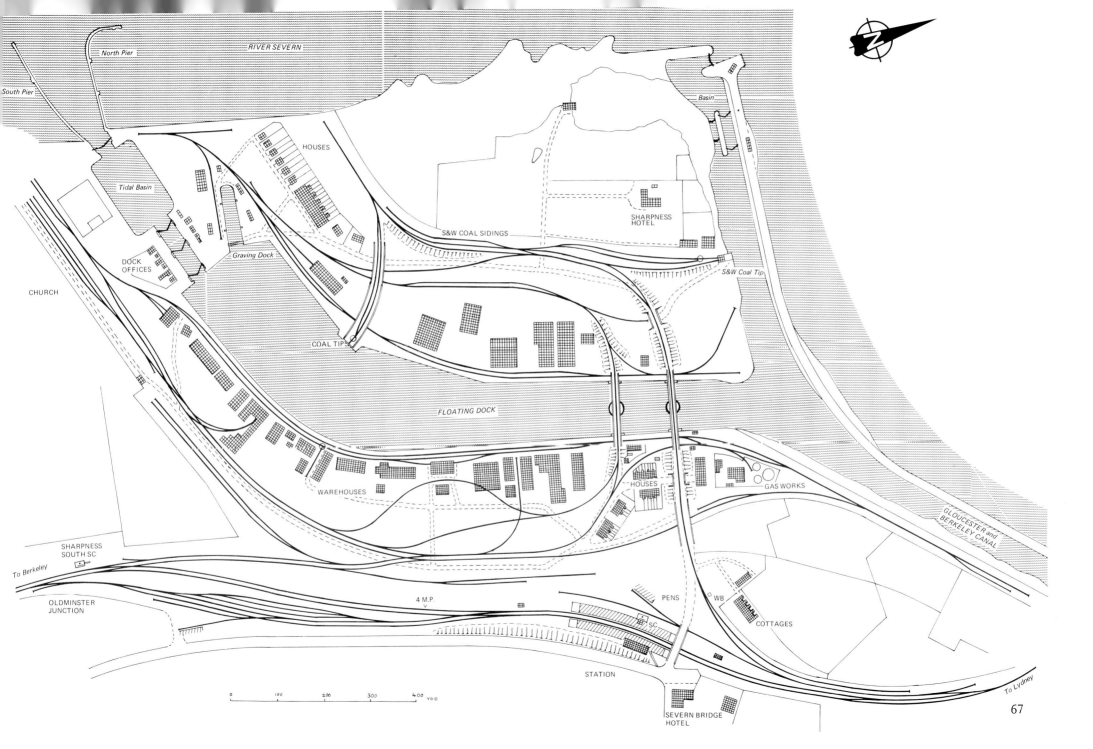

RIVER SEVERN

North Pier

South Pier

Tidal Basin

Basin

HOUSES

SHARPNESS
HOTEL

S&W COAL SIDINGS

DOCK
OFFICES

Graving Dock

S&W Coal Tip

CHURCH

COAL TIP

FLOATING DOCK

WAREHOUSES

HOUSES

GAS WORKS

GLOUCESTER and
BERKELEY CANAL

SHARPNESS
SOUTH SC

To Berkeley

OLDMINSTER
JUNCTION

4 M.P.

PENS

WB

COTTAGES

SC

STATION

To Lydney

SEVERN BRIDGE
HOTEL

0   100   200   300   400 YDS

67

SHARPNESS STATION BUILDING

The station building at Sharpness was a one-off design, and was built by the Severn Bridge Railway in 1879 for the new station which they shared jointly with the Midland Railway. The design owed little to S&W or MR practice, being a brick building with a hipped roof and having a shallow canopy over the platform. The rear wall was blank and lacked any relief to the plain brickwork, access to the building being from the platform. The roof was slated and the canopy was lead-covered. The station closed in 1964 and the building was demolished soon afterwards.

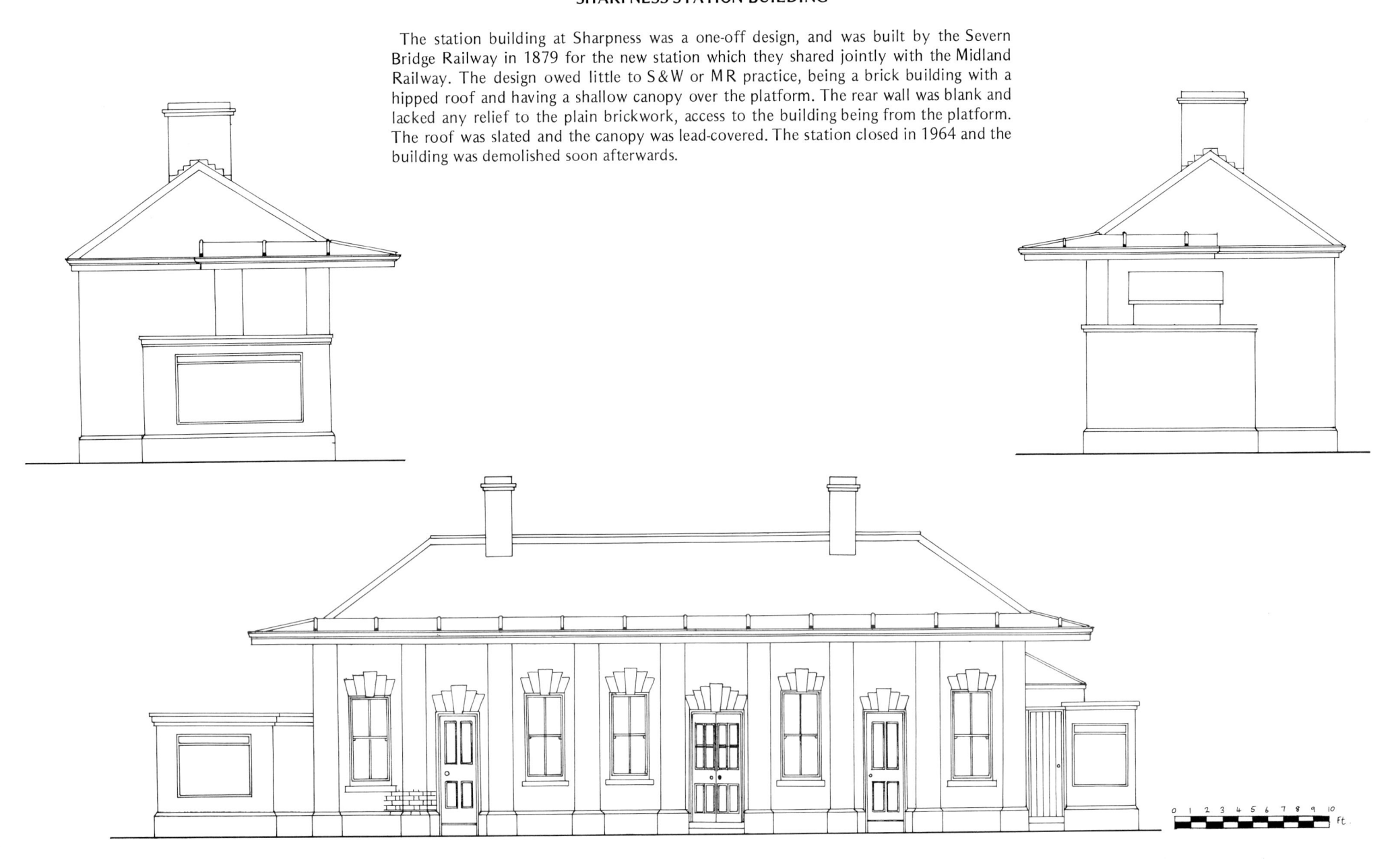

Sharpness
The station in the late 1930s. Little had changed except the GWR water-tower.

L&GRP

Sharpness
A 'Dean Goods' brings a South Wales diversion through the station, in March 1950. Note the LMS nameboards.

Real Photographs

Sharpness
The swing bridge across the dock at Sharpness, with the broken Severn Bridge seen beyond.

C. Maggs

A wagon built by Pickering & Co., circa 1903. The livery seems to be black with white lettering. Sharpness Chemical Company also ran rectangular tank wagons.

HMRS

BERKELEY

Opened: 2nd August 1875 (to freight); 1st August 1876 (to passengers)
Closed: 2nd November 1964 (to passengers)
Date of survey: 1890

Berkeley Station was the only intermediate station on the Midland Railway's Sharpness line of 1875. It was typically Midland, with attractive brick buildings and an early example of the standard MR wooden signal box, in this case on a brick base. The line was double track and the station had two platforms, joined by barrow crossings. North of the station the line crossed an attractive two arched brick bridge.

S&W trains began using the line in 1879 and from 1894, GWR trains were to be seen. However, the station retained its MR characteristics right up to its closure in 1964.

The line was singled on 26th July 1931, and the signal box was closed, while most sidings were not removed until 1958. Today one siding remains for the loading of atomic flasks from Berkeley Nuclear Power-Station. At the time of writing, 1980, much of the station was still intact.

Berkeley
The station, circa 1910, full of Midland Railway atmosphere.

Lens of Sutton

Berkeley
The station, circa 1960. Note the surviving Midland Railway platform barrows.

Lens of Sutton

A wagon built by the Gloucester Railway Carriage & Wagon Co. Ltd., in October 1896. The livery is chocolate, and it is lettered white, shaded black. The ironwork was probably black.

OPC Collection

BERKELEY

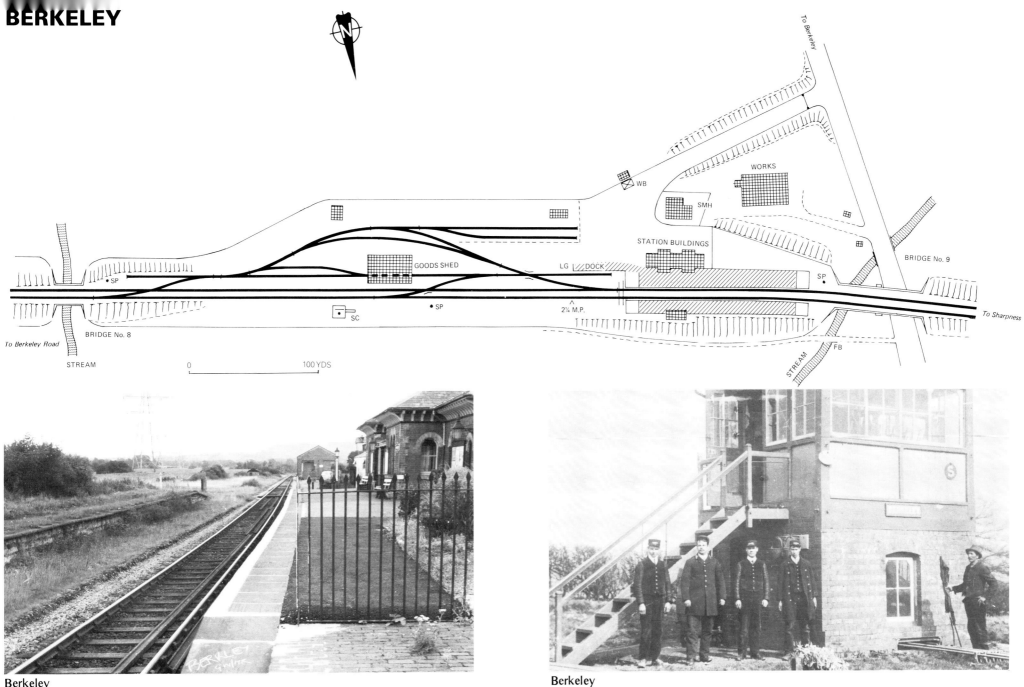

To Berkeley

WORKS

WB

SMH

STATION BUILDINGS

BRIDGE No. 9

GOODS SHED

LG DOCK

SP

SP

2¼ M.P.

To Sharpness

SC

SP

BRIDGE No. 8

STREAM

To Berkeley Road

STREAM

FB

0   100 YDS

Berkeley
Much had disappeared in the fifty years from 1910 to 1960.

Lens of Sutton

Berkeley
Berkeley signal box, circa 1915, with the station staff posing for a picture.

B. Edwards Collection

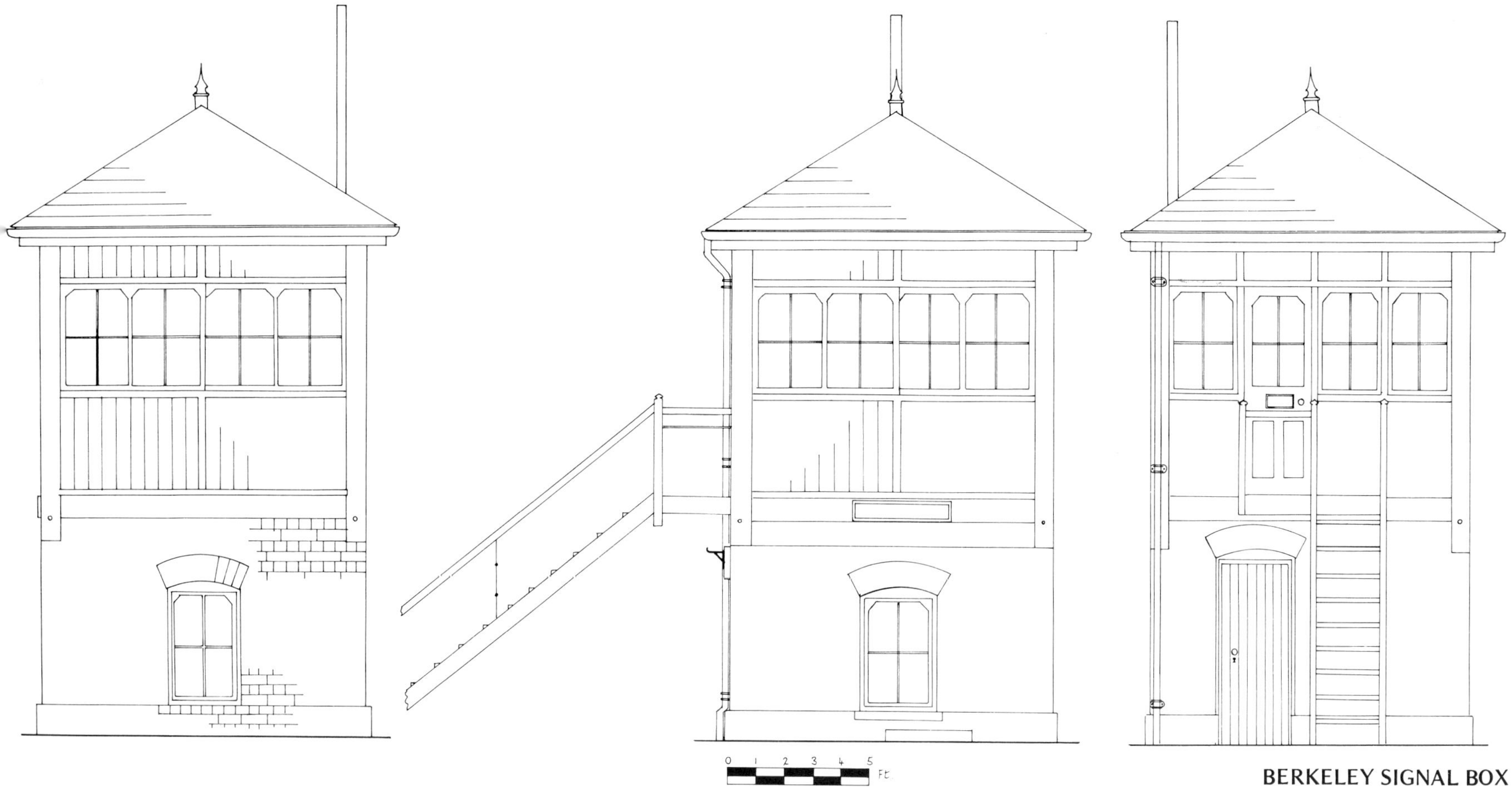

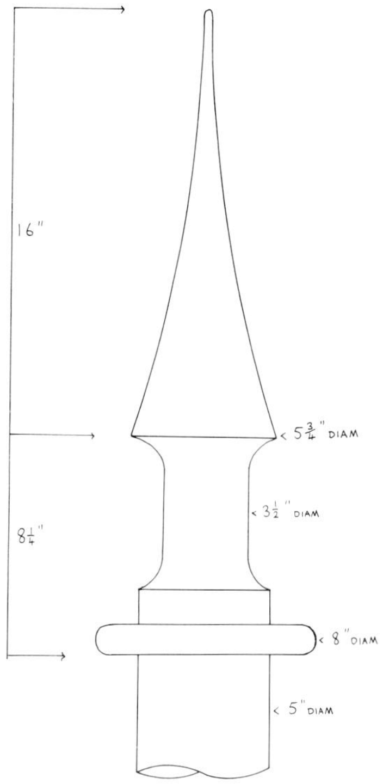

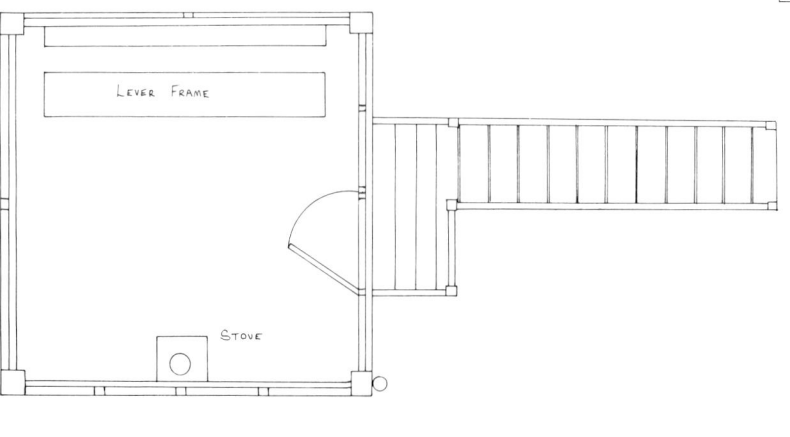

16"

8¼"

5¾" DIAM

3½" DIAM

8" DIAM

5" DIAM

BERKELEY SIGNAL BOX

LEVER FRAME

STOVE

0 1 2 3 4 5 Ft.

The signal box at Berkeley was interesting, being an example of the earliest Midland standard design of the mid-1870s. It was unusual in that it had a brick base, with a wooden upper section which came to typify the Midland Railway as much as its locomotives and coaches.

The box probably opened, with the station, in 1875, and lasted until 1931. The lower part of the box was turned into a permanent way hut and still survives. My thanks go to Brian Edwards for measuring this building and for providing the photograph of the cabin.

The box was square, and the brick section consisted of alternate layers of blue and red brick, with a door and two windows. The rear wall was blank. The wooden section, built of standard 10 ft. sections, had a hipped roof which was topped by a finial. This section was reached by a wooden stairway. Inside, the lever frame was at the front, with a shelf for the block instruments, and there was a stove at the rear. The windows on the front and at one side were of the sliding type.

The box differed from the slightly later standard cabins in a few respects. Apart from the brick base, the nameboard was blue with white lettering. For more details, reference should be made to the publication, *Midland Style* by the HMRS.

BERKELEY LOOP JUNCTION

Opened: 9th March 1908
Closed: 27th January 1963
Date of survey: 1920
Date of signalling plan: 1950

Berkeley Loop Junction was established when the GWR loop line from Berkeley Road South Junction was opened in 1908, to enable GWR trains to run south without reversing at Berkeley Road Station. This applied, especially, to Sunday diversions via the Severn Bridge, although the loop carried heavy goods traffic. Its building followed the granting of running powers over the MR main line as far as Yate South Junction.

The signal box was a standard GWR brick building and stood between the converging lines. It had twenty one levers and could be switched out when required. The layout was contracted in 1931, when the MR line was singled on 26th July, simplifying the signalling. The loop closed in 1963, increased axle loads having decreased the traffic using the Severn Bridge, 'Dean Goods' locomotives being the largest engines allowed over it. The signal box closed at the same time and has now been demolished.

Of course, through running had ceased with the damage to the Severn Bridge in 1960, with only dock traffic remaining from that date. This, of course, contributed greatly to the closure.

Berkeley
The signal box, as seen from a train on the GWR loop line.

Dr A. Dickins

Berkeley
Berkeley Loop Junction signal box.

P. Copeland

Berkeley
Class 4F No. 44560 passes the derelict signal box, in 1964, with grain from Sharpness and an atomic flask from Berkeley.

B. J. Ashworth

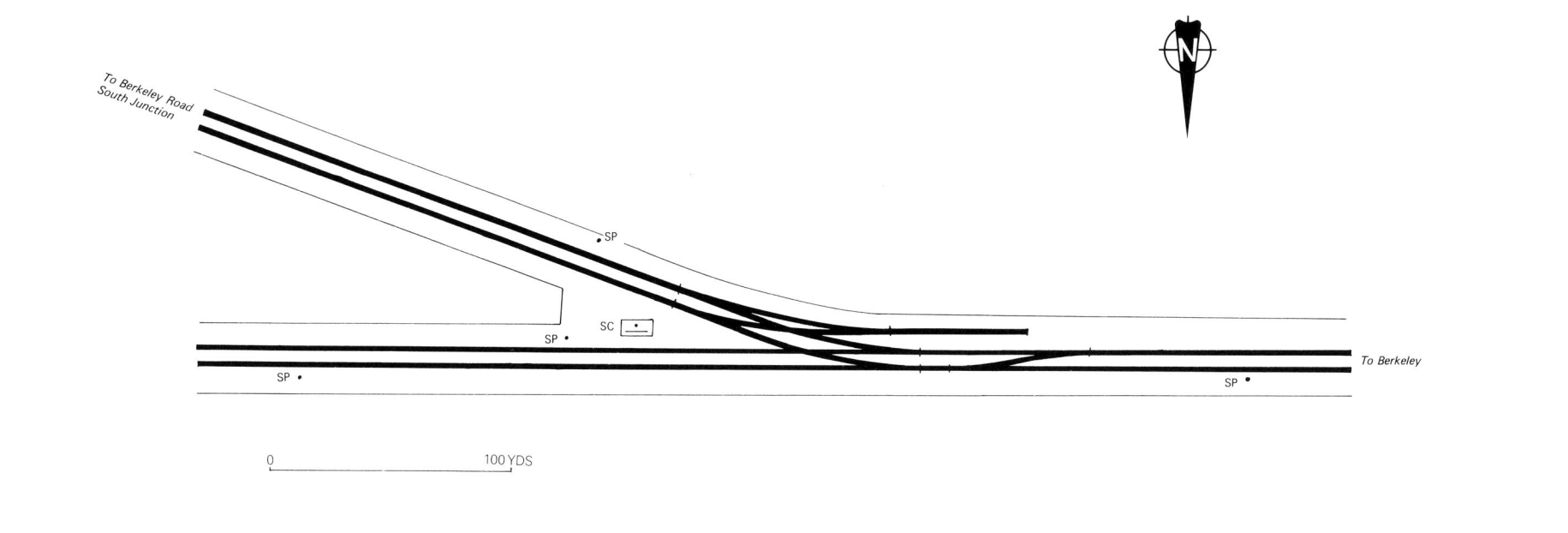

BERKELEY ROAD JUNCTION

Opened: 8th July 1844
Closed: 4th January 1965

Date of survey: 1920
Date of signalling plan: 1950

Berkeley Road was one of the six original stations on the broad gauge Bristol & Gloucester Railway, which was engineered by Brunel and opened in 1844. Snapped up by the MR in 1845, under the nose of the GWR, the line gave the MR access to the heart of GWR territory at Bristol and greatly changed Gloucestershire's railway history.

The station was typical Brunel in its architecture, and was most out of place on the Midland. It remained, as built, until 2nd August 1875, when the new branch was opened to Sharpness. Opened to passengers a year later, the branch joined the main line, north of the station, having separate platforms, a new station building and a footbridge, which was added in 1883. The MR signal box stood next to the junction and, at first, was a very tall cabin dating from about 1875. This was replaced, about 1890, by a standard cabin with a larger lever frame, this for the advent of interlocking and improvements to the signalling. In 1879, S&W trains began running through to the station, although the branch was MR-owned until 1894, when it was transferred to the S&W Joint Committee.

The branch was singled in 1931, and the passenger service ceased on 2nd November 1964, while the main line station closed on 4th January 1965. Although the branch remains, the station site has been cleared and only the station house remains.

Berkeley Road
The station, circa 1880, photographed by the Midland Railway, to show the new foot-bridge. Of interest are the slotted post signals, inside keyed track, and the original 1875 signal box which was replaced about 1890.

National Railway Museum

BERKELEY ROAD

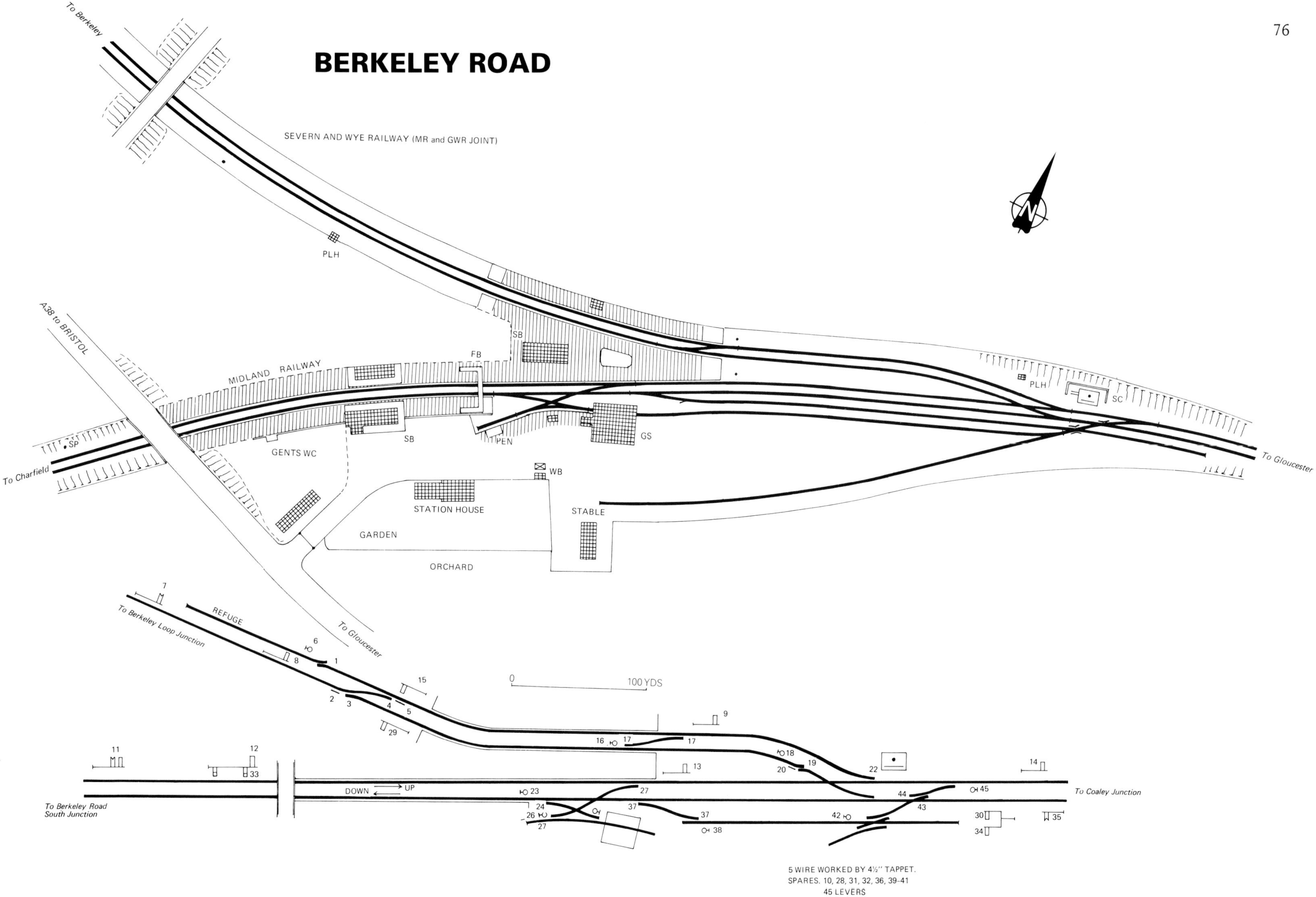

To Berkeley

SEVERN AND WYE RAILWAY (MR and GWR JOINT)

PLH

A38 to BRISTOL

SB

FB

MIDLAND RAILWAY

SB

GENTS WC

PEN

GS

To Charfield

SP

WB

STATION HOUSE

STABLE

GARDEN

ORCHARD

PLH

SC

To Gloucester

To Berkeley Loop Junction

REFUGE

To Gloucester

1

6

8

1

15

2

3

4

5

29

9

16

17

17

18

19

20

22

11

12

33

13

14

DOWN   UP

23

27

44

45

To Coaley Junction

To Berkeley Road
South Junction

24

26

27

37

37

42

38

43

30

35

34

0   100 YDS

5 WIRE WORKED BY 4½" TAPPET.
SPARES. 10, 28, 31, 32, 36, 39–41
45 LEVERS

Berkeley Road
S&W 0-6-0T *Friar Tuck* at the station between 1890 and 1894, with a brake third coach.
This delightful little engine typified the S&W fleet.

L&GRP

Berkeley Road
LMS Compound No. 1064 enters the station with a Gloucester train on 5th July 1947.
H. C. Casserley

Berkeley Road
In the 1960s, a 'Peak' class diesel connects with a 14XX 0-4-2T on the branch train.
H. Ballantyne

Berkeley Road
A view looking towards the junction from the branch platforms.

C. Maggs

Berkeley Road
A tidy looking station in 1932, showing the MR footbridge, and original Brunel awnings.
L&GRP

Berkeley Road
The Brunel goods shed, now demolished.

D. Ibbotson, Courtesy Brookside Photographic Services

A wagon built by the Gloucester Railway Carriage & Wagon Co. Ltd., in January 1934. The livery is black, and it is lettered in white.

OPC Collection

CRUMP MEADOW COLLIERY

Opened: 1829 (first rail connection 1855)
Closed: 1929
Date of survey: 1920

Crump Meadow was a large colliery by Forest standards. Situated to the west of Cinderford, the pit was served by a tramway until 1855, when a line was opened from the GWR line at Bilson Junction. In 1882, a line was built to the pit from Laymoor Junction, and when the mineral loop was built, another siding was built to the colliery, giving three separate rail outlets. The tramway remained in place for some time, after the opening of the railways, running east towards Cinderford, and crossing the GWR at Bilson Junction.

The colliery ceased operations in 1929, after which, the sidings were removed.

The method of working the various sidings was interesting. Empty trucks came in from the mineral loop and ran down to the colliery by gravity. The loaded trucks then ran, still by gravity, to the GWR line at Bilson Junction or to the S&W line at Laymoor Junction. Each of the sidings was actually owned by the colliery, although, no doubt, they were installed by the railway companies.

THE SEVERN & WYE MINERAL LOOP

The mineral loop was built by the S&W to the standard gauge, to give access to a number of collieries, and to connect, in the north, with the broad gauge line from Lydney, which was then relaid in mixed gauge. The line opened on 22nd April 1872, and the remainder of the S&W was not being standardized until 11/12th May. The line ran from Tufts Junction, via Drybrook Road, to join the broad gauge line at Wimberry, although, in later years, the Drybrook Road to Wimberry section was always considered as part of the main line.

The line was heavily used until the colliery closures of the early 20th century, but it was closed in 1942 for through traffic. In March 1951, the Blakeney road bridge was demolished and track was lifted north of Pillowell, this being completed in September 1956. The final section, from Pillowell to Tufts Junction, was closed on 30th November 1957. The line was 6½ miles long and it never carried passenger trains.

Crump Meadow Colliery
All that remains of the colliery, in 1947.

P. Copeland

To Drybrook Road

N

A

A

A

A

SP

WASTE TIP

moor Junction

SCREENS

WB

SHAFT

TANK

CHY

HOUSES

To Tufts Junction

B

B

0   100 YDS

FOREST RIDES

B

B

To Bilson Junction

Tramway to Cinderford

Map labels:
- To Woorgreen Colliery
- To Coleford
- To Cinderford
- To Tufts Junction
- GF
- 16MP
- GF
- GF
- To Drybrook Road

0   100 YDS

WOORGREEN COLLIERY SIDING

Opened: 1903
Closed: 1912 (removed 1938)
Date of survey: 1905

This siding served a very short-lived pit, Woorgreen Colliery, which opened in 1903. In 1912 the pit closed, although the siding was not lifted until 1938. This pit was remarkably unsuccessful, even by Forest standards, where closures were commonplace.

LIGHTMOOR COLLIERY

Opened: 1823-1835 (Railway opened 22nd April 1872)
Closed: 8th June 1940
Date of survey: 1880

Lightmoor Colliery was owned by the influential Crawshay family and was one of the largest in the Forest. Established in the 1820s, and soon expanded, a tramway connected it to the Forest of Dean Tramway, until that line was converted into a railway in 1854. A line was then built from the pit to Bilson Junction, being a private standard gauge line operated by the colliery with small tank locomotives.

With the opening of the S&W loop line, which passed the colliery, in 1872, a new outlet was available and sidings were soon laid.

The colliery closed on 8th June 1940, although the buildings remained in use by the army until 1945 and they quickly became derelict. The loop line closed in 1951 and was lifted soon after, the Lightmoor Railway having closed with the pit.

The plan shows the colliery in 1880, with the S&W sidings and the connection to the private line. The layout had changed little over the years. The old tramway remained in place, although, probably, unused except for the dumping of waste.

The second plan shows the junction with the loop line as they were about 1920, and is taken from the GWR survey. The GWR plan does not show the colliery itself, but this was, no doubt, very much as on the main plan.

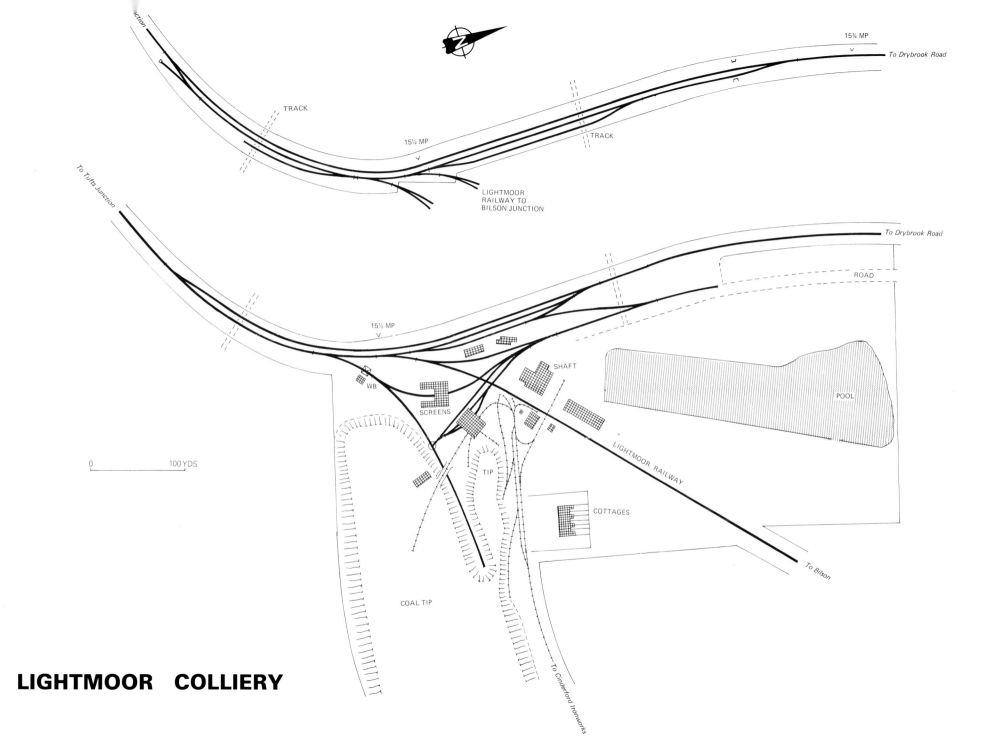

To Drybrook Road

15¾ MP

TRACK

15½ MP

TRACK

LIGHTMOOR
RAILWAY TO
BILSON JUNCTION

To Tufts Junction

To Drybrook Road

ROAD

15½ MP

SHAFT

WB

POOL

SCREENS

LIGHTMOOR RAILWAY

TIP

0   100 YDS

COTTAGES

To Bilson

COAL TIP

To Cinderford Ironworks

LIGHTMOOR COLLIERY

Lightmoor Colliery
The colliery in the 1940s, with the mineral loop seen on the right.

P. Copeland

Acorn Patch Depot
The entrance to the sidings, showing the ground frame cabin.

P. Copeland

A wagon built by the Gloucester Railway Carriage & Wagon Co. Ltd., in October 1899. The livery is lead grey, and it is lettered white, shaded black. It has black ironwork.

OPC Collection

ACORN PATCH DEPOT

Opened: 1943
Closed: 16th June 1953
Date of survey: 1944

  This quaintly-named army ammunition depot was short lived, and its origins are interesting. It came into being in 1943, when an isolated location for ammunition storage was required. The actual explosives were stored in Mosely Green Tunnel. In fact, the track was removed from the line in 1942, but it was reinstated and a section of Forest was cleared for the three sidings and the approach road. A ground frame controlled the junction with the mineral loop.

  The mineral loop was severed, in 1951, and its southern end and the depot, redundant in peace time, was closed. Trains were run to clear stocks, the last one leaving on 16th June 1953. Both loop and the depot then closed and the track was removed in 1956.

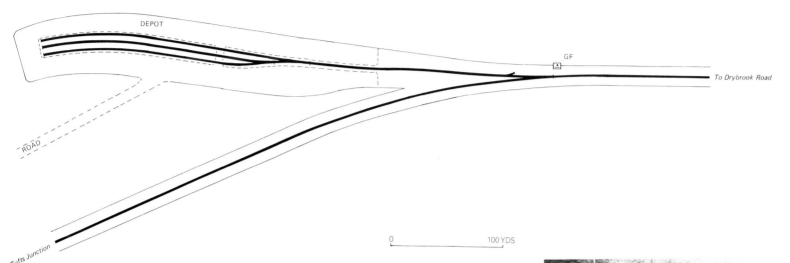

DEPOT

GF

To Drybrook Road

ROAD

0   100 YDS

To Tufts Junction

Acorn Patch Depot
The ammunition depot in 1946.

P. Copeland

NEW FANCY COLLIERY

Opened: circa 1840. Railways: 25th May 1868 (Central line)
22nd April 1872 (S&W Mineral Loop)
Date of surveys: 1910 (Colliery); 1920 (Junction)

New Fancy was one of the largest of the Forest collieries, and production was well established when the Central line reached it in 1868. This was the northern terminus of the line and involved a reversal to reach Awre Junction. The line relied on the pit for its very existence and when the S&W mineral loop was opened, past the pit, in 1872, it cut off the Central line's main traffic source to a trickle. In 1878, it was cut back to Howbeach Sidings. Meanwhile, the S&W prospered, with New Fancy coal reaching Lydney via Tufts Junction. Two loop sidings were laid at the junction with the mineral loop together with a water-tower and a water crane at the south end.

The colliery remained in production until 1944, by which time only 50 tons of coal a week were being transported. The site was used, for a time, as a dump for old tramway wagons. The rail connection was removed in August 1944.

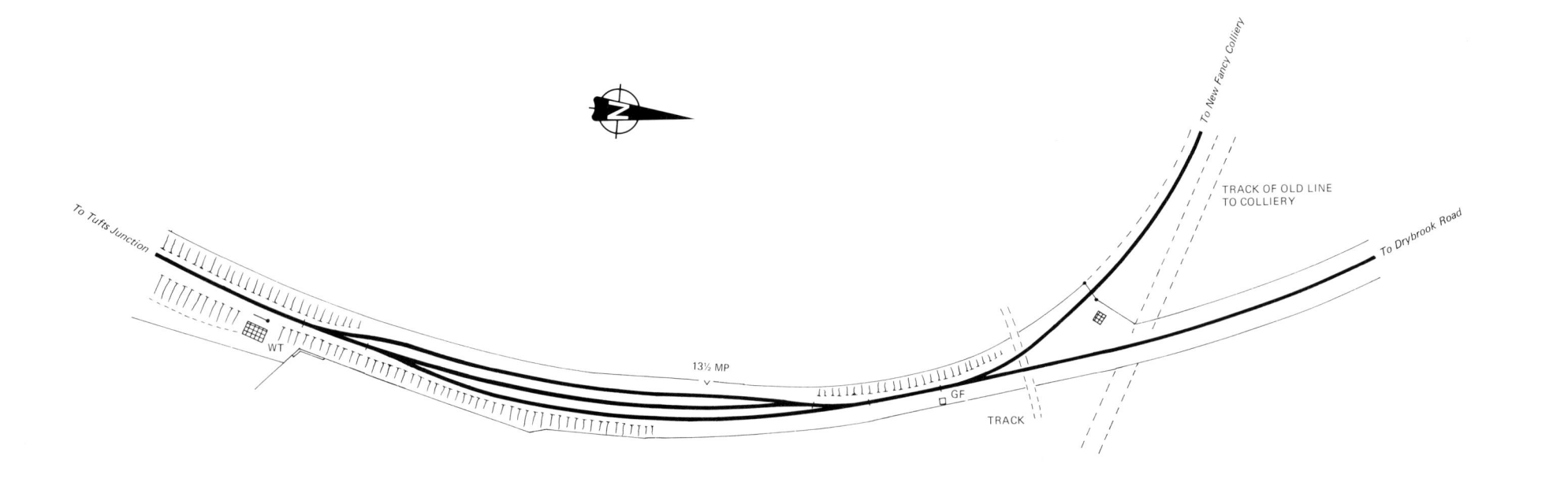

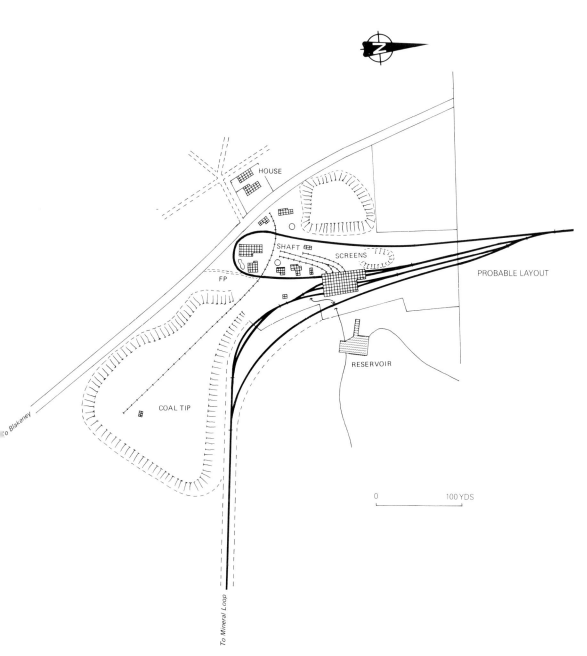

HOUSE

SHAFT

SCREENS

FP

PROBABLE LAYOUT

RESERVOIR

COAL TIP

To Blakeney

To Mineral Loop

0   100 YDS

New Fancy Colliery
The junction of the colliery line in 1944.

P. Copeland

New Fancy Colliery
The colliery pictured soon after closure.

P. Copeland

SECTION 4

COLEFORD JUNCTION TO COLEFORD (SEVERN & WYE RAILWAY)
AND COLEFORD TO WYESHAM JUNCTION (GREAT WESTERN RAILWAY)

Coleford was served by two lines, as befitted the Forest capital, and they approached from opposite directions. From the east came the S&W which opened to freight on 19th July 1875, and to passengers on 9th December of the same year. The line was steep, much at 1 in 30, and sharply curved, but it carried heavy traffic.

In 1883, the GWR arrived from Monmouth, via Wyesham Junction, on the Wye Valley line, opening on 1st September. The two termini were side by side, but the antagonism of the two companies kept co-operation to a minimum.

The section of the GWR line from Whitecliff Quarry to the Wye Valley Junction, closed on 31st December 1916 as part of the wartime scrap drive, and never reopened. Traffic from the quarry ran over the S&W line. This lost its passenger trains on 6th July 1929, but the stone trains remained until 11th August 1967. Official closure came on 2nd October 1967.

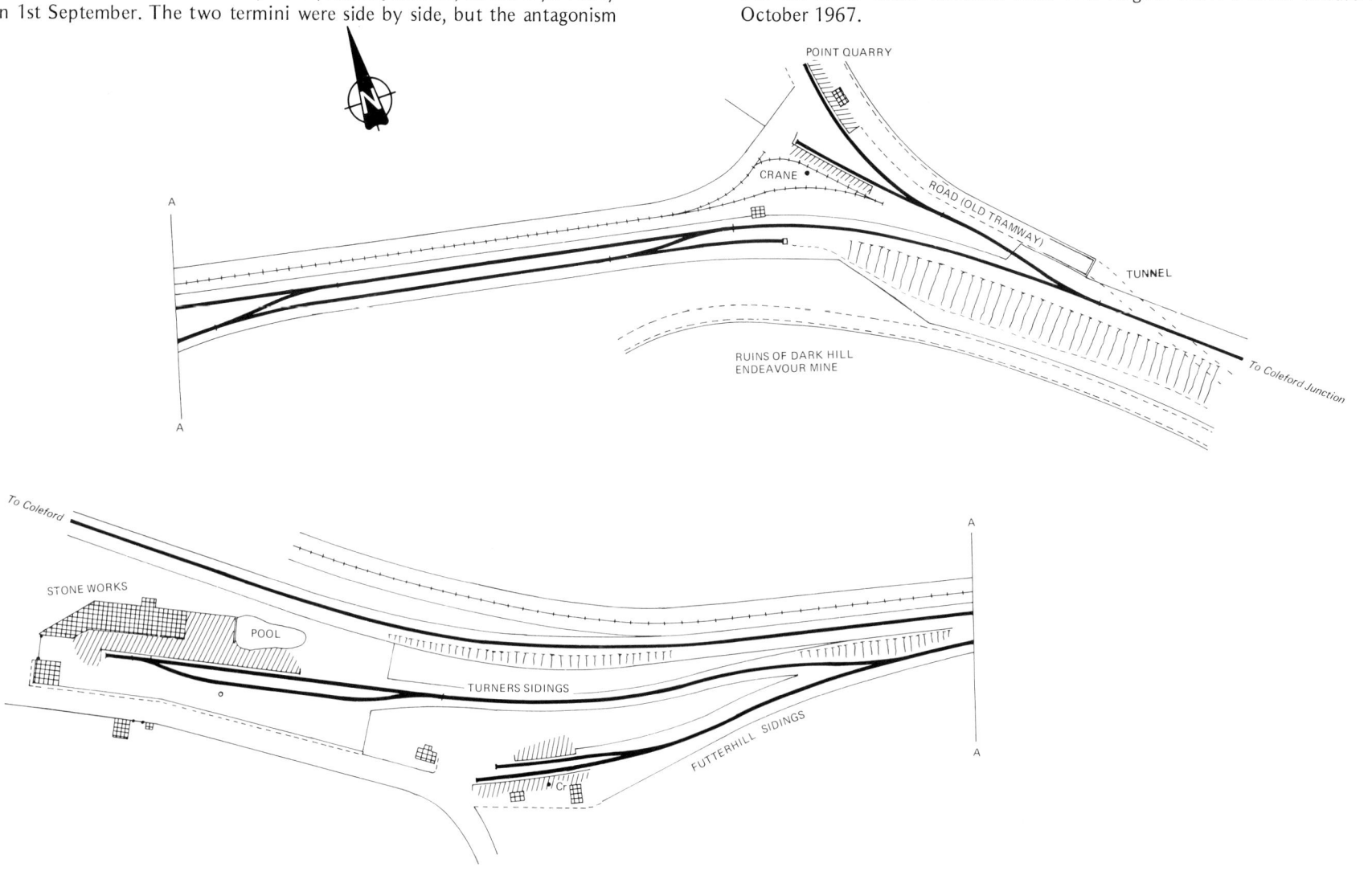

FUTTERHILL SIDINGS AND POINT QUARRY SIDING

Opened: 19th July 1875 (Soon after the line opened)
Closed: Removed in 1957 after a period of disuse
Date of survey: 1900

These sidings were really three separate entities, although it is convenient to consider them together. Approaching from Coleford Junction, Point Quarry Siding diverged on the right, 1 mile 35 chains from the junction, and a tunnel under the line showed the route of the former tramway. To the left of the line were Futterhill Sidings, dropping away from the climbing main line to terminate at the roadside, serving Turner's Stoneworks and Futterhill Brickworks. A loop once served Darkhill Level Pit, long since closed, this being an area covered with industrial ruins. The sidings closed, in 1957, after being little used for some time.

MILKWALL AND THE SLING BRANCH

Opened: 19th July 1875 (to freight); 9th December 1875 (to passengers)
Closed: 1st May 1944 (to freight); 6th July 1929 (to passengers)
Date of survey: 1900

Milkwall was the only intermediate station on the S&W's Coleford line, opening in December 1875 for the start of passenger trains. There was one short platform, with a wooden station building and a goods shed. These were later replaced by brick buildings, after a fire. The station was very basic, with a loop and one siding serving, as it did, a featureless area. It closed on 6th July 1929, and freight ceased on 1st May 1944. The station building, dated 1924, survived for many years.

Interest was added by the fact that this was the junction for the Sling mineral branch, which ran south to Sling Siding, replacing a tramway route. The line terminated at loading docks, and was 52 chains long. A loop near the junction served an ochre works, and the track then ran, unfenced, through bleak country to the wharf, once used for iron ore. In 1924, the engineering works of F. Watkins was established at the railhead. The line remained in situ until its closure in 1967.

Milkwall
A very small station but, nevertheless, beautifully maintained — Milkwall Station, circa 1905.

P. Copeland Collection

Milkwall
A view of the Sling branch, near the junction at Milkwall.

P. Copeland

MILKWALL

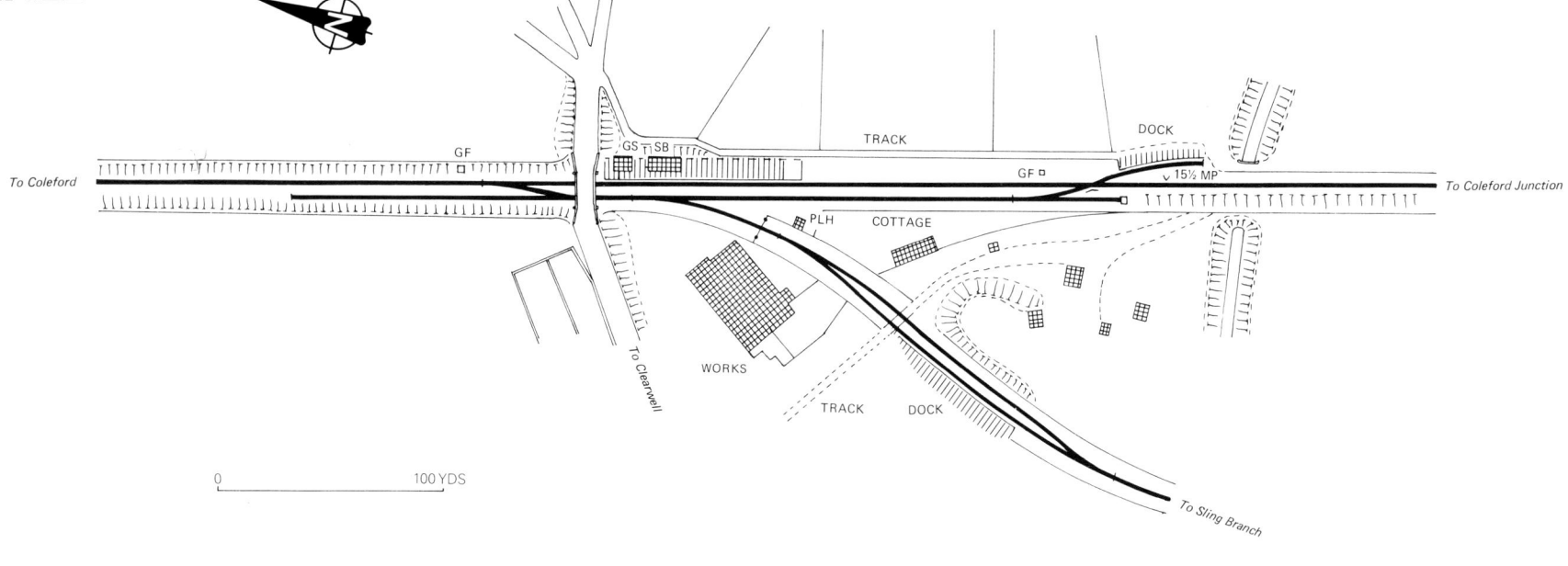

To Coleford

GF

GS SB

TRACK

DOCK

GF

15½ MP

To Coleford Junction

To Clearwell

PLH

COTTAGE

WORKS

TRACK

DOCK

To Sling Branch

0   100 YDS

SLING BRANCH

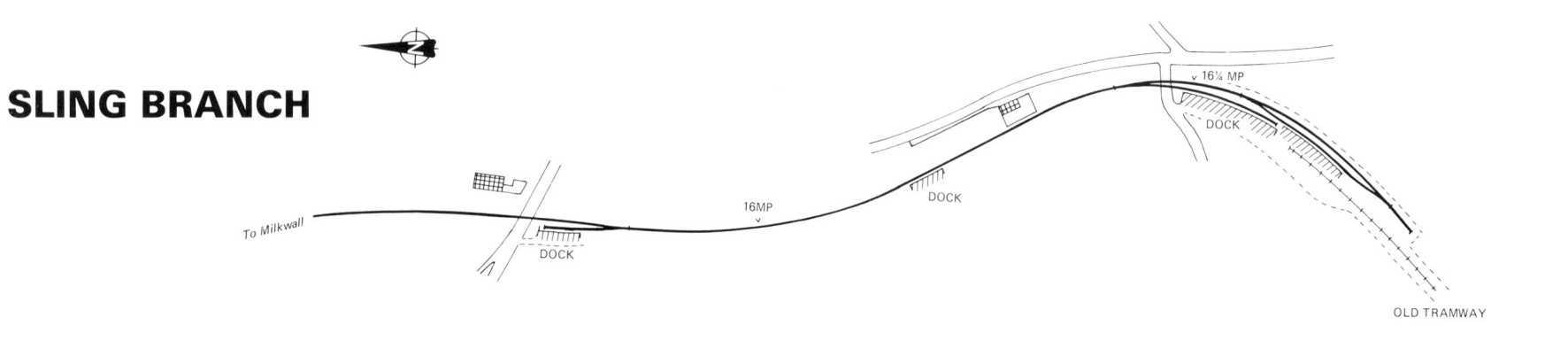

To Milkwall

16MP

DOCK

DOCK

16¼ MP

DOCK

OLD TRAMWAY

0   100 YDS

Milkwall
Stone from Whitecliff Quarry passes Milkwall behind 0-6-0PT No. 8745.

R. Blencowe

Milkwall
A view from the overbridge.

P. Copeland

Sling
The terminus of the Sling branch, in 1946.

P. Copeland

Milkwall
A view looking towards Coleford.

Lens of Sutton

Coleford
The S&W station, circa 1910, showing the original wooden station building.

Lens of Sutton

COLEFORD S&W AND GWR STATIONS

Opened: S&W Station — 9th December 1875 (to passengers)
19th July 1875 (to freight)
Closed: 6th July 1929 (to passengers)
11th August 1967 (to freight)
Opened: GWR Station —1st September 1883 (to passengers and freight)
Closed: 31st December 1916 (to passengers)
11th August 1967 (to freight)

Date of survey: 1910

The two Coleford stations are treated together, as they were so close to one another and were physically connected.

The S&W branch was the first to open, in July 1875, and the station opened to passengers on 9th December the same year. A compact single-platformed terminus, it comprised the usual wooden station building, a wooden goods shed, a loading bank, a cattle pen and a small water-tower which served a water crane. The station building was burnt down in 1914 and was replaced by a very plain brick-built structure.

The GWR line arrived from Monmouth in 1883, after much delay, and a terminus was built adjacent to the S&W Station, facing the other way. A joint station would have seemed logical, but the companies were barely on speaking terms, and it took some years to arrange the eventual transfer siding, which involved four reversals, making it all but useless. Remarkably, this absurd arrangement was not altered until 1951.

The GWR Station had a single curved platform with a standard design station building of brick, and a wooden signal box on a brick base. There were sidings behind the platform and a large two storey brick-built goods shed, with loading banks, etc. There was a loop line which ran around the platform.

The lines were worked as separate entities. In the 1880s, MR trains reached Coleford, giving this market town a service by three independent companies! This could not last, and the GWR line closed, west of Whitecliff Quarry, in 1916. The S&W line closed to passengers in 1929 and, finally, in 1967, to all traffic. Little now remains on the site (1980) except the GWR goods shed.

Coleford
The station, fifty years later, looking rather different.

Lens of Sutton

Coleford
The arrival of a railtour at Coleford, circa 1960.

Lens of Sutton

Coleford
A special at Coleford S & W station, on 23rd June 1962.

S. Clarkson

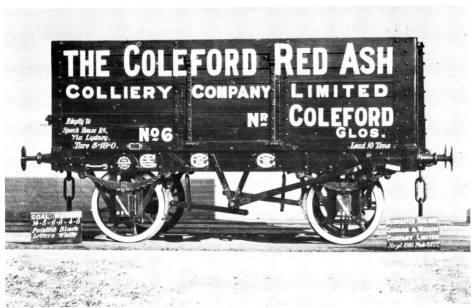

A wagon built by the Gloucester Railway Carriage & Wagon Co. Ltd., in September 1950. The livery is black, and it is lettered in white.

OPC Collection

A wagon built by the Gloucester Railway Carriage & Wagon Co. Ltd., in November 1893. The livery is black, and it is lettered in white.

OPC Collection

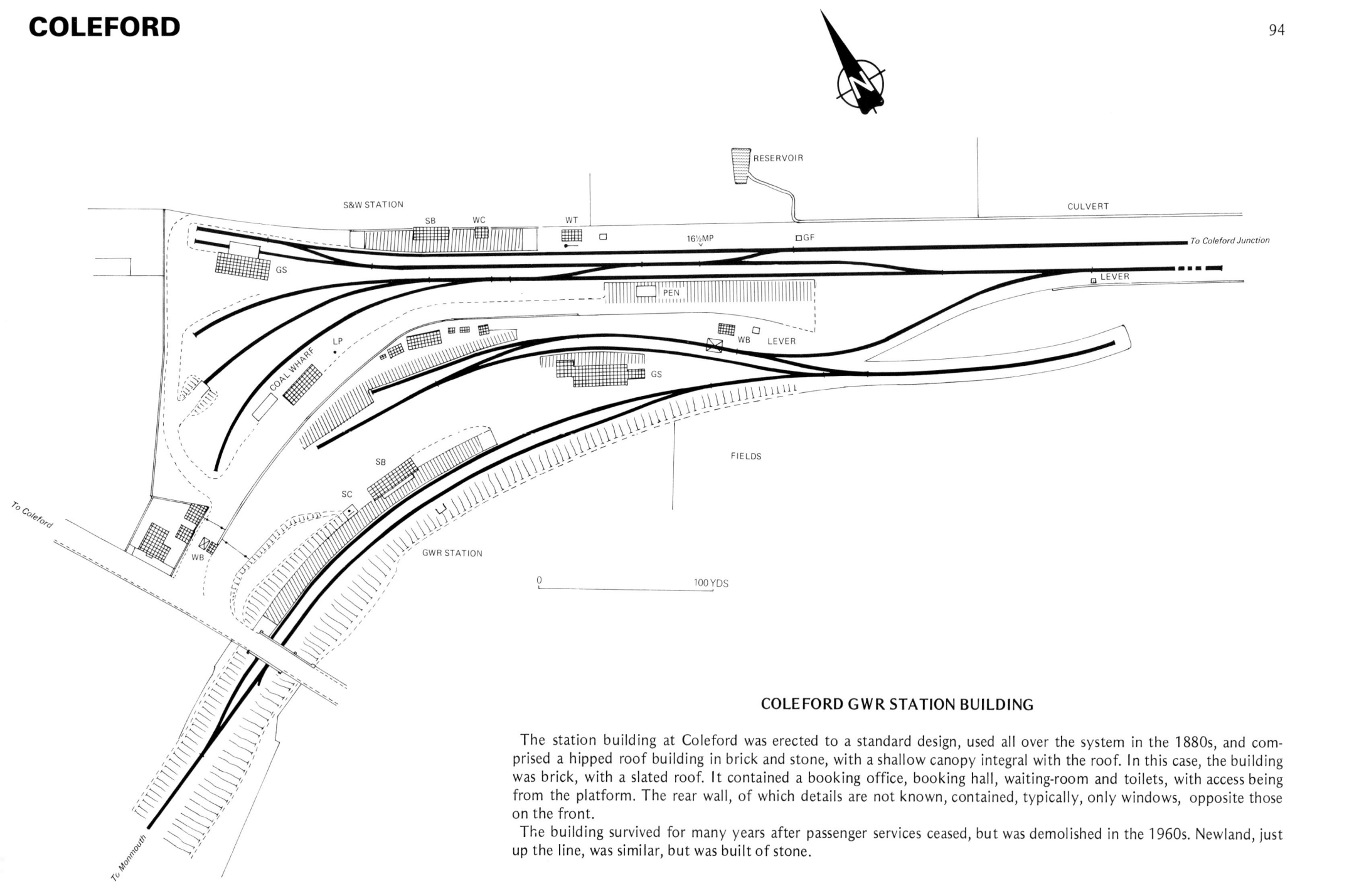

RESERVOIR

S&W STATION

SB WC WT

CULVERT

16½ MP

GF

To Coleford Junction

GS

PEN

LEVER

WB LEVER

LP

COAL WHARF

GS

SB

FIELDS

To Coleford

SC

WB

GWR STATION

0   100 YDS

To Monmouth

COLEFORD GWR STATION BUILDING

The station building at Coleford was erected to a standard design, used all over the system in the 1880s, and comprised a hipped roof building in brick and stone, with a shallow canopy integral with the roof. In this case, the building was brick, with a slated roof. It contained a booking office, booking hall, waiting-room and toilets, with access being from the platform. The rear wall, of which details are not known, contained, typically, only windows, opposite those on the front.

The building survived for many years after passenger services ceased, but was demolished in the 1960s. Newland, just up the line, was similar, but was built of stone.

0 1 2 3 4 5 6 7 8 9 10 11 12
Ft

Coleford
The station, circa 1910, as seen from the road bridge.

Lens of Sutton

Coleford
A view looking towards Newland, circa 1960.

Lens of Sutton

Coleford
The main buildings, still unchanged, in the early 1950s.

Lens of Sutton

Coleford
The large brick goods shed, with a far newer shed buulding in front, as seen from the platform.

Lens of Sutton

WHITECLIFF LIME KILN SIDING

Opened: Date unknown
Closed: 11th August 1967
Date of survey: 1890

This siding diverged from the Coleford to Monmouth line to serve a lime kiln at the western end of the short Whitecliff Tunnel. The importance of the siding was considerable, as when the line closed in 1916, the stretch to Coleford was retained, traffic passing on to the S&W line, including the four reversals at Coleford. By that time, the quarry had become more important than the kiln, providing road-stone, railway ballast, etc., but this shows the early layout for the kiln only, the quarry being behind it on the hillside. A number of changes later occurred in the layout, notably in 1930, but unfortunately plans of the later layout have not been traced.

Whitecliff Quarry was the reason for the retention of the Coleford line until 1967. Traffic was then taken to the Parkend railhead by road, but since 1976, the whole journey has been by lorry.

The opening date for the siding is uncertain, but it was probably laid, with the line, in 1883.

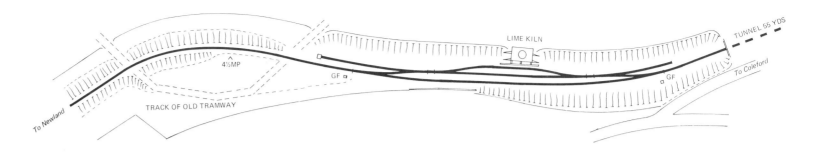

Whitecliff Lime Kiln Siding
Diesel-hydraulic Paxman shunter, No. D9555 shunts the siding on 23rd March 1967.
R. Blencowe

An early dumb-buffered wagon built by the Gloucester Railway Carriage & Wagon Co. Ltd., in September 1886. The livery is stone and it is lettered in black.
OPC Collection

NEWLAND

Opened: 1st September 1883
Closed: 31st December 1916
Date of survey: 1900

This station was some distance away from the village of Newland, and was the only intermediate station on the GWR's Coleford to Monmouth branch, which joined the Wye Valley line at Wyesham Junction. The station opened, with the line, in an area known as the Cherry Orchard, and had a passing loop and two platforms, with solid stone buildings to standard GWR designs. The signal box and platform shelter were of wood. A loop siding served a loading bank and a goods shed, with a crane. Another siding ran to a dock for the loading of iron ore.

The service was always meagre, and it ceased during World War I, in 1916, the line being removed for scrap. The buildings survived intact for many years after its closure.

This delightful little station would make a charming and unusual model, if operation was a secondary consideration.

Newland
A view looking along the trackbed between the platforms, showing the main buildings, which were then being demolished. These buildings had last been used over 50 years previously!

Lens of Sutton

To Berry Hill

IRON ORE WHARF · Cr · GS

SC

^ 2¾MP

SMH

PLH

SB · FOUNTAIN

OIL

SP

To Monmouth

To Redbrook

To Coleford

To Coleford

0   100 YDS

SECTION 5

SERRIDGE JUNCTION TO LYDBROOK JUNCTION (SEVERN & WYE RAILWAY)

The S&W Lydbrook branch opened to mineral traffic on 26th August 1874. Passenger services commenced on 23rd September 1875 to connect with the GWR's Ross to Monmouth trains.

A 'mountaineering' line, it climbed from Serridge Junction and served several pits along its route to Upper Lydbrook Station. At Lower Lydbrook, it was on a high ledge above the valley, which it crossed by way of the attractive Lydbrook Viaduct, 390 ft. long. At one time, the branch carried heavy iron ore traffic to South Wales and also some excursion trains, but in later years, traffic was almost nil.

Closure to passengers came on 6th July 1929, and to freight, it came more progressively. From 1st January 1953, the freight trains terminated at Upper Lydbrook, the line remaining as a siding at the junction. The line closed beyond Mierystock on 30th January 1956 and the remaining section closed on 21st November 1960.

Lydbrook Viaduct was demolished in May 1966.

MIERYSTOCK SIDINGS

Opened: 1915
Closed: 5th August 1960
Date of survey: 1920

These sidings were laid in 1915 to serve the colliery screens of the newly-reopened Arthur & Edward Colliery. A siding had existed on this site since 1874, but this was of a simpler nature, serving the aptly-named Speculation Colliery. The new sidings led up a gradient, alongside the main line, which soon entered Mierystock Tunnel, which was 242 yards in length. The colliery lines crossed above the tunnel, running to the screens where the coal was loaded. The traffic was considerable and closure was only agreed on 31st July 1956 owing to the poor condition of the track. In fact, trains ran until total closure on 5th August 1960 when the line to Serridge Junction also closed. Track lifting was completed in February 1962.

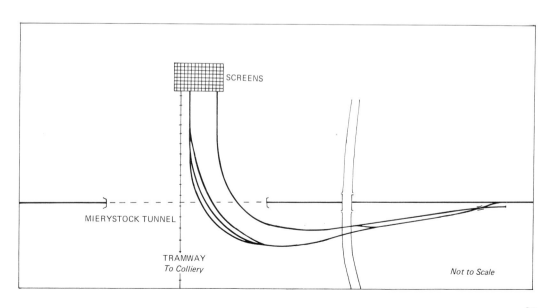

SCREENS

MIERYSTOCK TUNNEL

TRAMWAY
To Colliery

Not to Scale

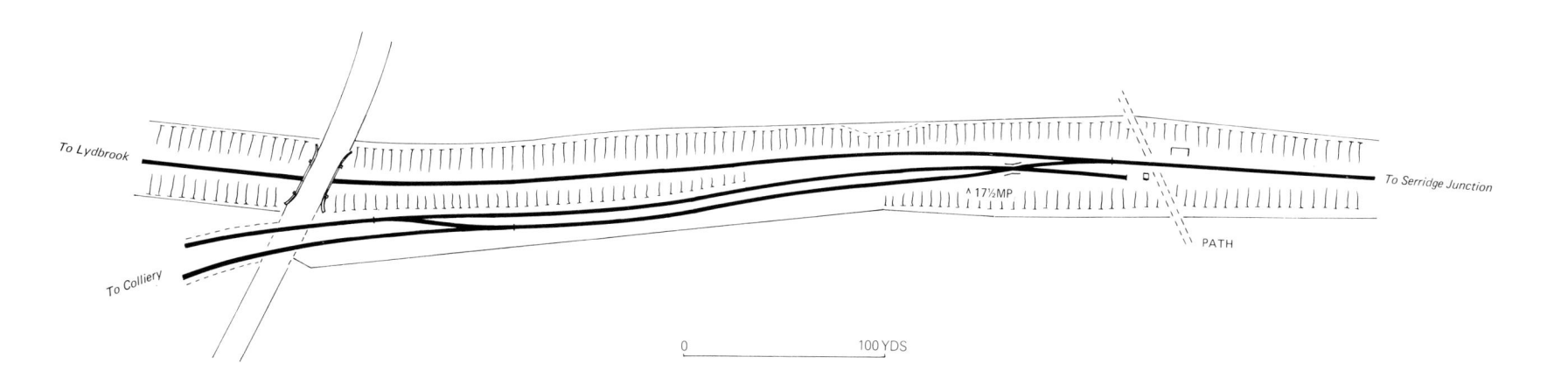

To Lydbrook

To Serridge Junction

^ 17½MP

PATH

To Colliery

0   100 YDS

Mierystock
Mierystock Tunnel.

S. Clarkson

Mierystock
The road bridge at Mierystock, with the tunnel beyond.

S. Clarkson

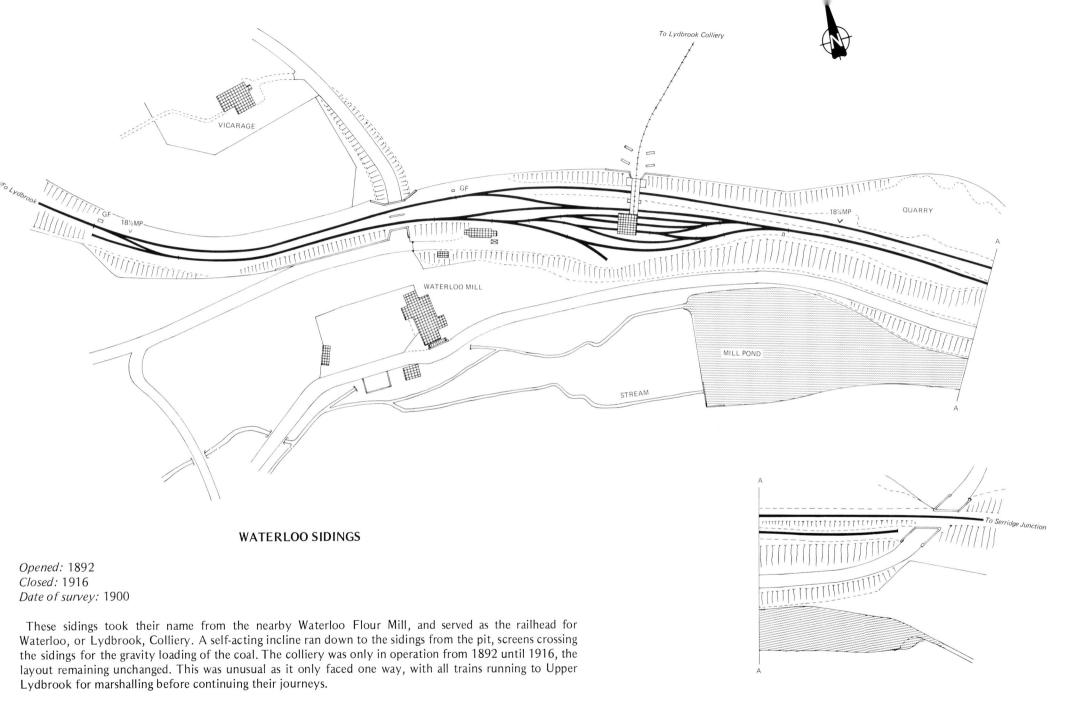

WATERLOO SIDINGS

Opened: 1892
Closed: 1916
Date of survey: 1900

These sidings took their name from the nearby Waterloo Flour Mill, and served as the railhead for Waterloo, or Lydbrook, Colliery. A self-acting incline ran down to the sidings from the pit, screens crossing the sidings for the gravity loading of the coal. The colliery was only in operation from 1892 until 1916, the layout remaining unchanged. This was unusual as it only faced one way, with all trains running to Upper Lydbrook for marshalling before continuing their journeys.

UPPER LYDBROOK

Opened: 26th August 1874 (to freight); 23rd September 1875 (to passengers)
Closed: 30th January 1956 (to freight); 6th July 1929 (to passengers)
Date of survey: 1910

Upper Lydbrook was the station for the higher parts of the strung out village of Lydbrook, opening in 1875 for the start of passenger services. There were two platforms, with the usual wooden station building and goods shed, and a level crossing, passing the platform ends, which formed a connection between them. A large GWR signal box stood on the 'down' side near the crossing. This had replaced an S&W cabin in 1912 which, in turn, replaced two earlier boxes in 1892.

The goods yard was originally two sidings, but in 1908, a scissors crossing was put in and a siding was added for the traffic from Waterloo Pit. The main line passed through Coles Rock Tunnel, which was 1 chain in length, and which emphasized the rocky and hilly nature of the terrain. It was very attractive, but not ideal railway country.

Passenger traffic ceased in 1929 and goods continued until 1956, the station building being used, for some time, as a private house.

Upper Lydbrook
The station, in 1949, showing the GWR signal box.

P. Copeland

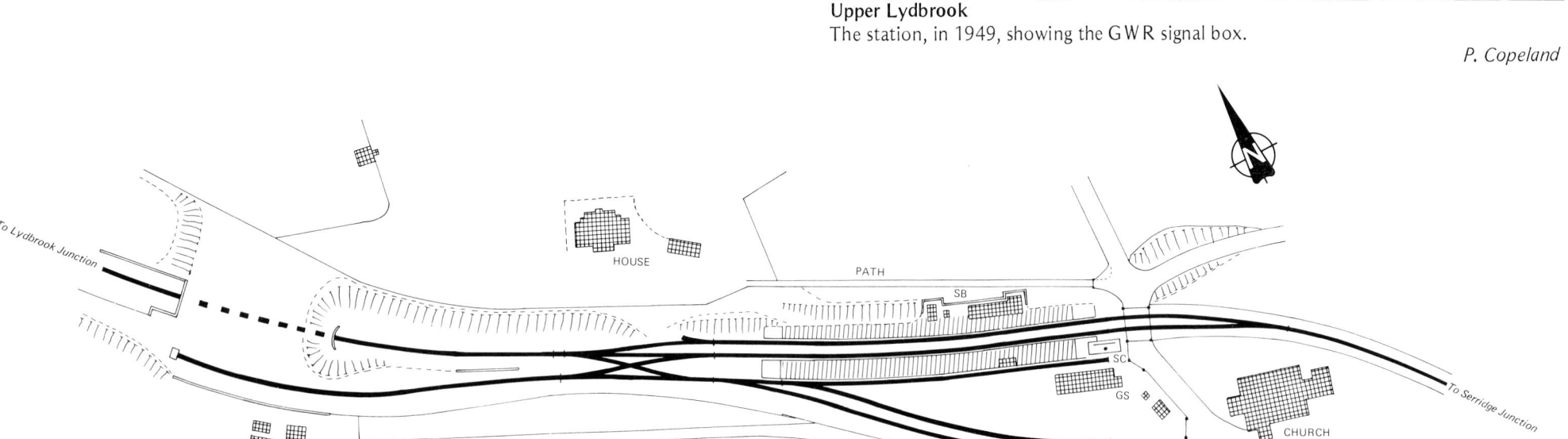

UPPER LYDBROOK STATION BUILDING

The station building at Upper Lydbrook typified the S&W structures provided in 1875. All were similar, although no two were alike.

The building was basic, containing a booking hall/waiting-room, a booking office and toilets. It was built of wood, with horizontal planking and a slated roof. The chimneys were of brick, as was the base on which the building stood. One chimney was parallel to the rear wall and the other, at 45 degrees to it.

0 1 2 3 4 5 Ft.

Upper Lydbrook
The scene in the 1960s, as seen from the level crossing. The station was surrounded by steep hills.

Lens of Sutton

Upper Lydbrook
A view looking towards the crossing, after closure of the station.

LOWER LYDBROOK

Opened: 23rd September 1875 (to passengers); 26th August 1874 (to freight)
Closed: 1st April 1906 (to passengers); 1st January 1953 (to freight)
Date of survey: 1900

Lower Lydbrook
Lydbrook Viaduct, with the village beneath.

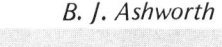

B. J. Ashworth

Lower Lydbrook Station and sidings were situated high on the hillside above Lower Lydbrook itself, at the end of the lofty and graceful Lydbrook Viaduct, which crossed the valley above the village. The layout was basic, the station being a single platform with a small wooden shelter, closing as early as 1906. The sidings were laid to serve the wire and tinplate works in the valley floor, and a long incline ran down to these works. Shortened in 1901, it was removed in 1938, having been worked by locomotives. These locomotives worked down bunker first, to keep the water over the firebox. A siding served a weighbridge and this completed the facilities.

A signal box stood between the viaduct and the platform and was later replaced by two ground frames which closed in 1938. The line closed on 1st January 1953, although the viaduct remained until 1966.

There was a severe speed limit over Lydbrook Viaduct from the outset, 6m.p.h. being the initial limit, reducing to 5m.p.h.

LOWER LYDBROOK

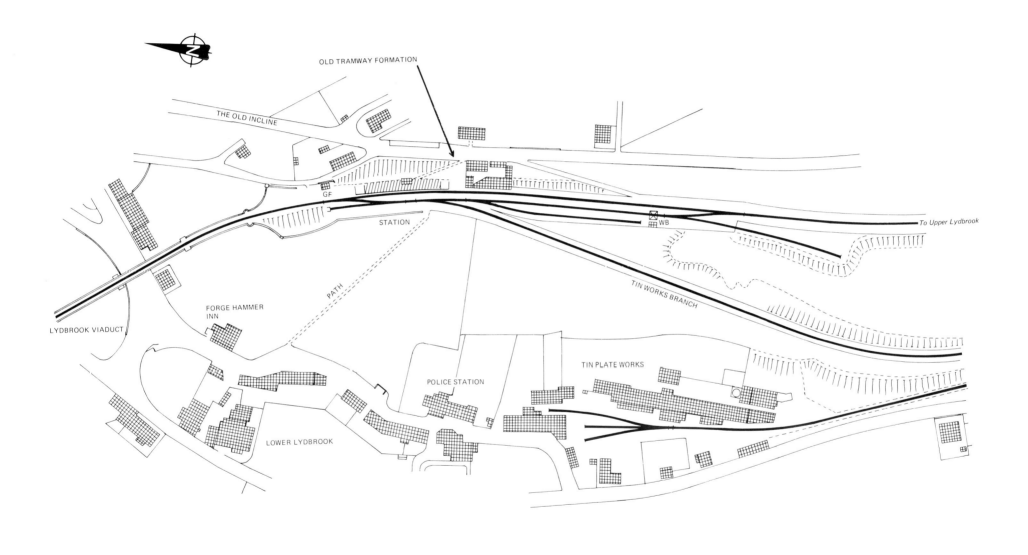

OLD TRAMWAY FORMATION

THE OLD INCLINE

GF

STATION

PATH

FORGE HAMMER
INN

LYDBROOK VIADUCT

POLICE STATION

TIN PLATE WORKS

TIN WORKS BRANCH

WB

To Upper Lydbrook

LOWER LYDBROOK

0   100 YDS

Lower Lydbrook
Lower Lydbrook, circa 1925. The railway runs along the hillside, and a pannier tank and some wagons can be seen. The incline came down past the tall chimney seen on the right.
P. Copeland Collection

Lower Lydbrook
The viaduct as seen from the village.
S. Clarkson

Lower Lydbrook
A view looking across the viaduct, in 1962.
S. Clarkson

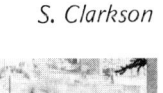

Lower Lydbrook
The viaduct, as seen from the junction.
S. Clarkson

Lydbrook Junction

The station, after closure to passengers, showing the GWR platforms.

Lens of Sutton

LYDBROOK JUNCTION

Opened: S&W trains — 26th August 1874 (to freight)
23rd September 1875 (to passengers)
Closed: S&W trains — 1st January 1953 (to freight)
6th July 1929 (to passengers)
Date of survey: 1900
Date of signalling plan: 1950

Lydbrook Junction came into being when the S&W branch was built in 1874 to join the GWR's Ross to Monmouth line. A junction station was built and S&W passenger services commenced on 23rd September 1875. Lydbrook Junction was, at first, the terminus of the service from Lydney, although the line was later treated as a branch.

Each line had two platforms, with the station building being situated on the island between the converging routes. The second S&W platform was not required and was used for loading goods, as only the GWR had a goods shed. A water-tower stood at the end of this platform and the GWR signal box was opposite; a brick structure replaced an earlier wooden box.

There were sidings, belonging to the S&W, beyond the junction, and crossovers in both directions. The principal through traffic, in the early years, was iron ore from Cinderford to South Wales, but, in later times, very little traffic of any nature came off the S&W line. The S&W passenger trains ceased in 1929 and freight came to an end in 1953, although the line was retained as a siding.

The GWR passenger trains ended on 5th January 1959 and the signal box closed on 26th February 1961, freight trains remaining until 1965. The GWR line had opened in August 1873.

Bicknor Siding was opened by the S&W in 1888 owing to a lack of siding space at the junction. It was used for loading goods, until its removal with the line.

Lydbrook Junction

A view looking towards the junction, showing the large GWR signal box.

Lens of Sutton

LYDBROOK JUNCTION

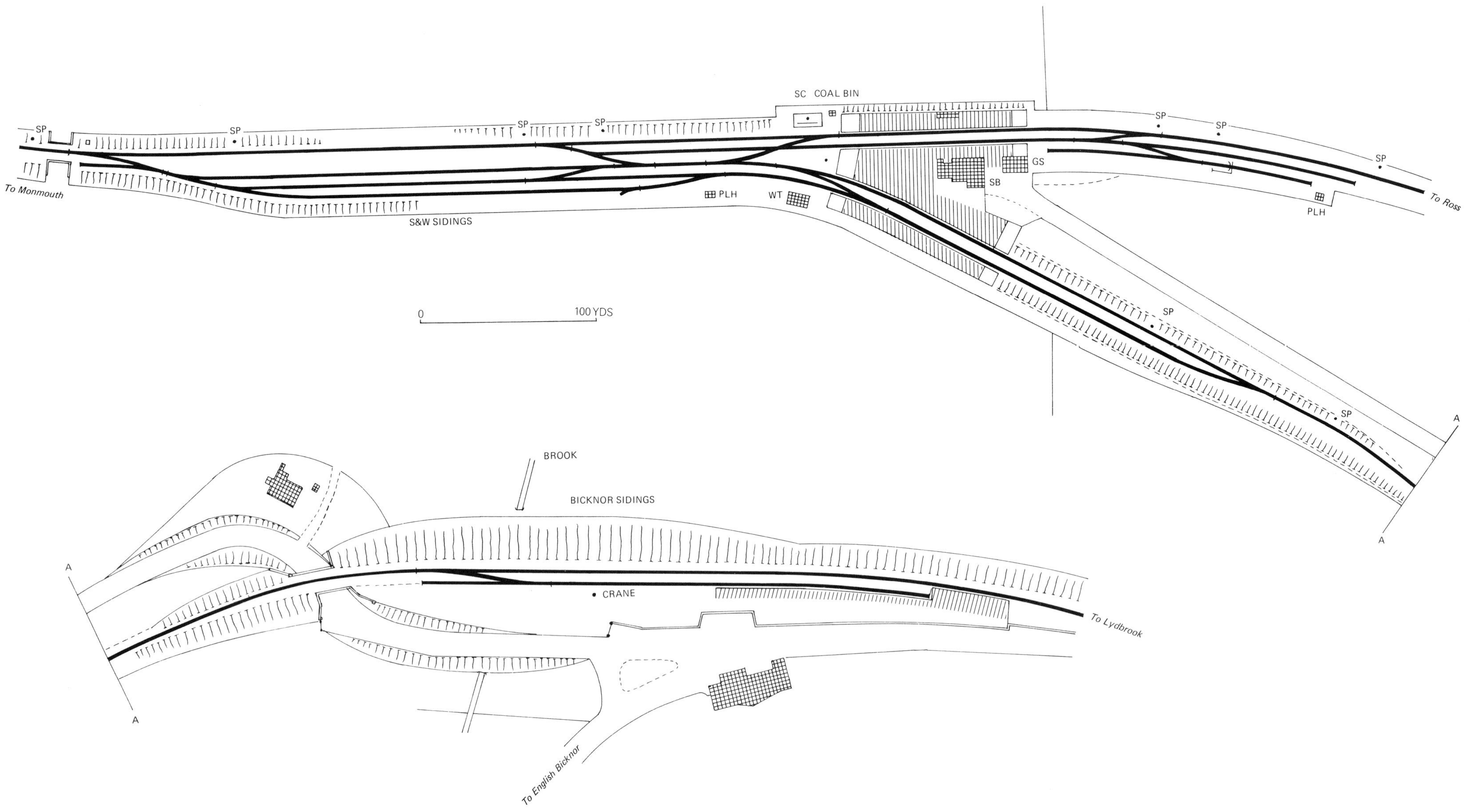

SC COAL BIN

SP

SP

SP

SP

SP

SP

SP

SP

SP

SP

SP

To Monmouth

GS

SB

S&W SIDINGS

PLH

WT

PLH

SP

SP

To Ross

A

A

0   100 YDS

BROOK

BICKNOR SIDINGS

CRANE

A

A

To Lydbrook

To English Bicknor

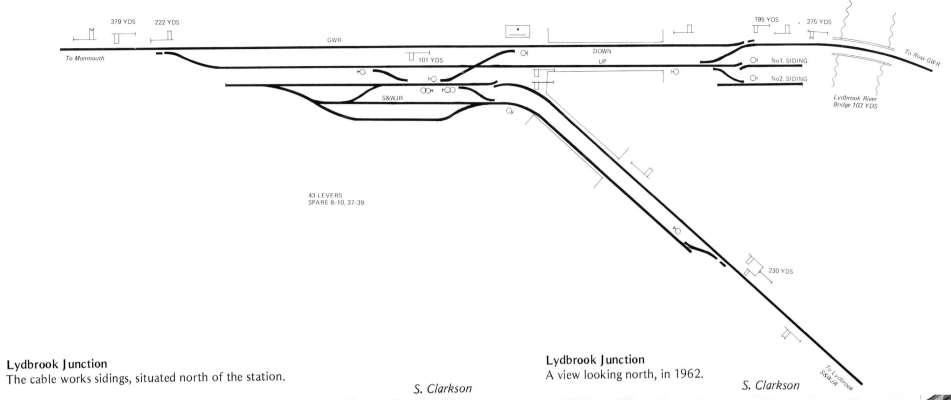

379 YDS 222 YDS

195 YDS 275 YDS

GWR

To Monmouth

DOWN

UP

101 YDS

S&WJR

To Ross GWR

No1. SIDING

No2. SIDING

Lydbrook River
Bridge 103 YDS

43 LEVERS
SPARE 8-10, 37-39.

230 YDS

To Lydbrook
S&WJR

Lydbrook Junction
The cable works sidings, situated north of the station.

S. Clarkson

Lydbrook Junction
A view looking north, in 1962.

S. Clarkson

Lydbrook Junction
On the right is the S&W platform. By this time the station building had been extended.

Lens of Sutton

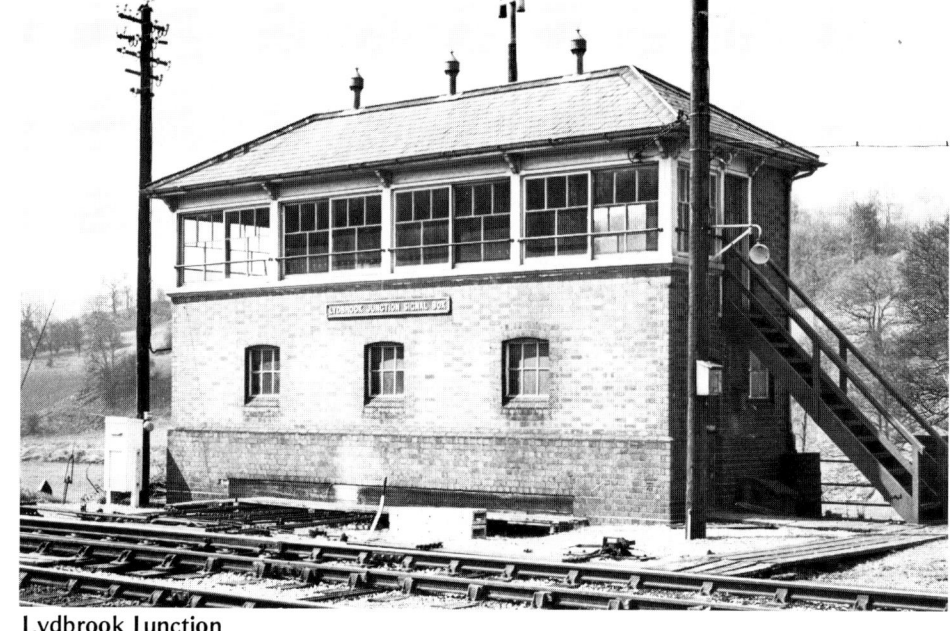

Lydbrook Junction
A 1962 view.

S. Clarkson

Lydbrook Junction
The main station building.

Photomatic

Lydbrook Junction
The scene on the last day of passenger services, 3rd January 1959.

S. Clarkson

SECTION 6

The Central line was proposed to tap the resources of the area between the S&W and Forest of Dean lines; an upland area dotted with collieries poorly served by the tramways and railways. The line was to run from Awre Junction on the South Wales Railway main line, which had been taken over by the GWR on 1st August 1863. Foxes Bridge Colliery was to be the terminus, and the line would serve New Fancy and other pits in the area.

The line was built, and eventually opened, after a great deal of trouble, on 25th May 1868, running only as far as New Fancy Colliery. Traffic was brisk, but the S&W mineral loop was built soon after and when it opened in 1872, it cut right across the Central line at New Fancy. The S&W built a line to the colliery and, at once, all the traffic went to Lydney, leaving the Central line high and dry. The Foxes Bridge extension was never built and, in 1878, only ten years after opening, the line was cut back to Howbeach Sidings, serving a few small pits.

Traffic ceased beyond Blakeney in 1921, (official closure was in 1932), and the line finally succumbed on 10th August 1959, the last revenue-earning trip having been on 29th July 1949.

The Central line's sad history must be almost unique in railway history.

AWRE JUNCTION

Opened: 19th September 1851
Closed: 10th August 1959
Date of survey: 1926
Date of signalling plan: 1960

Awre Junction existed as a simple station from the opening of the SWR main line in 1851, becoming a junction when the Central line was opened on 25th May 1868. This was always a freight only line, so the station was little affected.

There were two short platforms with typical small SWR gabled buildings and a level crossing which joined the platforms. Beyond this, was the physical junction, the Central line having loop sidings and a siding serving a small dock and cattle pen. A signal box, having twenty eight levers and dating from 1909, stood between the lines, and it replaced an earlier box which had been sited opposite.

The branch traffic ceased on 29th July 1949, but it was used for wagon storage until its official closure on 10th August 1959. On the same date, the station closed to goods and passenger traffic. The signal box was closed on 30th December 1973 and the site has now been cleared.

Awre Junction
'Awre for Blakeney', circa 1910.

Lens of Sutton

AWRE JUNCTION

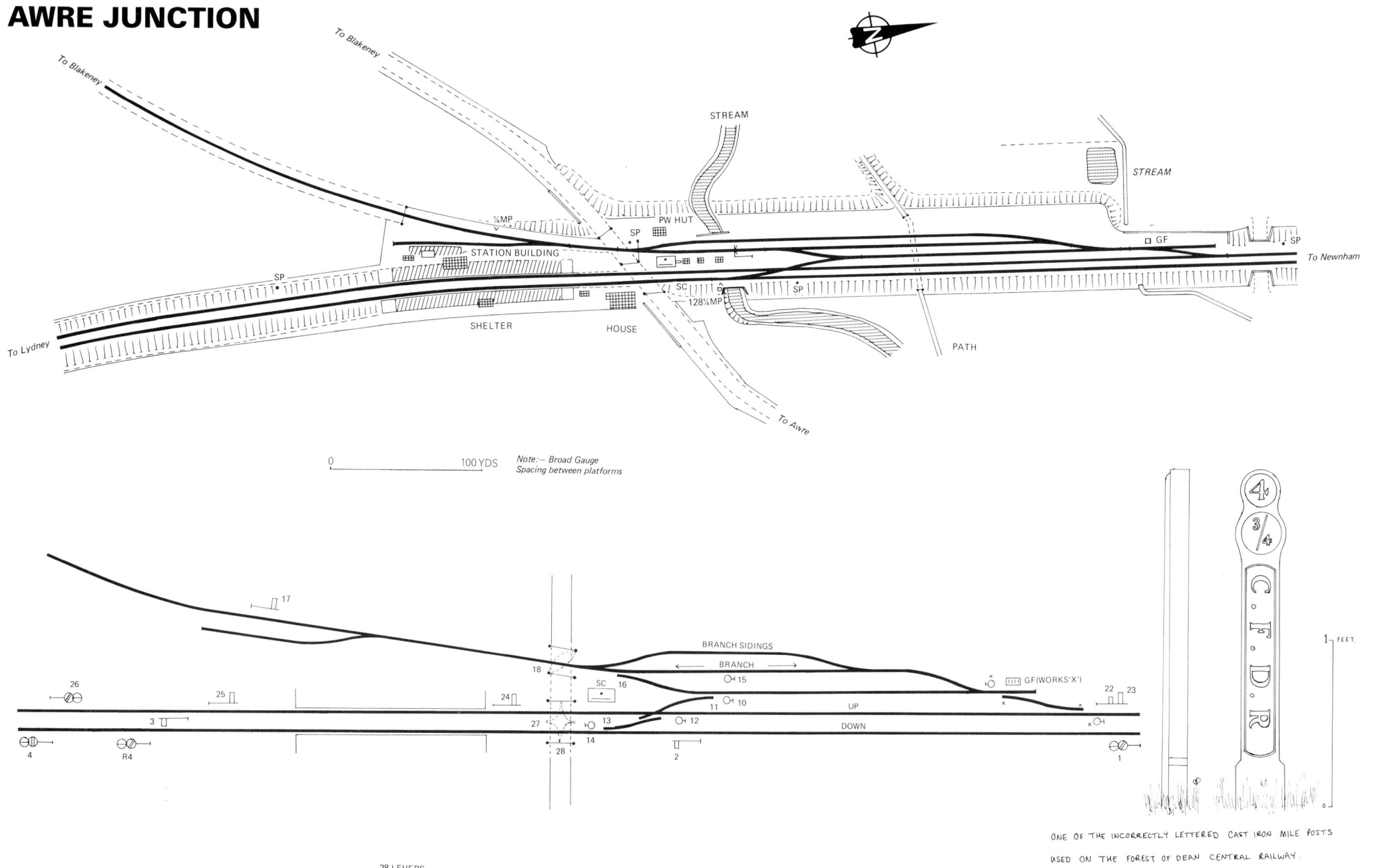

To Blakeney

To Blakeney

STREAM

STREAM

¼MP

PW HUT

SP

GF

SP

STATION BUILDING

To Newnham

SP

SP

SC

SP

128¼MP

SHELTER

HOUSE

PATH

To Lydney

To Awre

0   100 YDS

Note:– Broad Gauge
Spacing between platforms

17

BRANCH SIDINGS

BRANCH

18

15

SC   16

GF (WORKS 'X')

26

25

24

22   23

3

11   10

UP

27   13

12

DOWN

4   R4

28   14

2

1

28 LEVERS
SPARES: 7,9,19-21.

4
¾
C.F.D.R

1 FEET.

ONE OF THE INCORRECTLY LETTERED CAST IRON MILE POSTS
USED ON THE FOREST OF DEAN CENTRAL RAILWAY.

Awre Junction

Awre remained almost pure South Wales Railway well into the 1950s.

P. Copeland

Awre Junction

A view from the signal box.

P. Copeland

Awre Junction

The station in 1947.

P. Copeland

Awre Junction

A 'down' goods passes the signal box in this view, seen from the 'up' starting signal, in 1947.

P. Copeland

BLAKENEY GOODS STATION

Opened: 25th May 1868
Closed: 29th July 1949
Date of survey: 1900

The goods station at Blakeney was a mile north of Awre Junction, and the Central line should never have gone any further! The station consisted of a wide platform with a stone goods shed and a crane, served by a single siding. This was the end of the line from 1921 onwards, (official closure being in 1932), until closure in 1949, although the line to the south was used for wagon storage for another ten years.

North of Blakeney, the A48 road was crossed by a bridge with a 30 ft. metal span, while a little further on was Blakeney Viaduct, comprising eight stone arches and two metal spans. The stone section still remains.

Blakeney
Blakeney goods station in 1947.

P. Copeland

Blakeney
The bridge across the A48 road. The 30 ft. girder span was typical of bridges on the line. The bridge was demolished in 1959.

P. Copeland

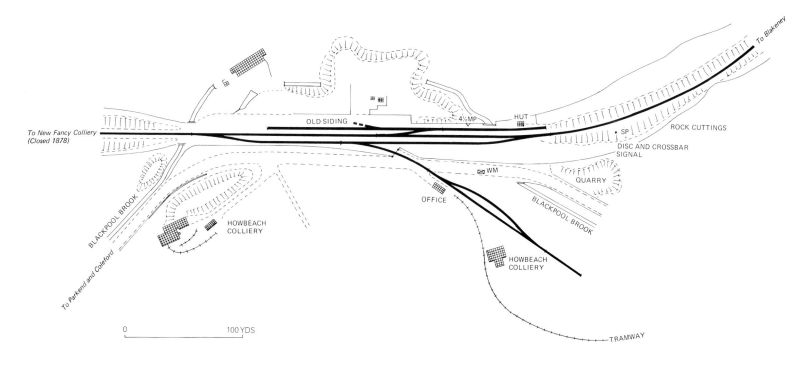

To New Fancy Colliery
(Closed 1878)

To Parkend and Coleford

BLACKPOOL BROOK

OLD SIDING

4½MP

HUT

To Blakeney

ROCK CUTTINGS

SP

DISC AND CROSSBAR
SIGNAL

QUARRY

BLACKPOOL BROOK

WM

OFFICE

HOWBEACH
COLLIERY

HOWBEACH
COLLIERY

TRAMWAY

0   100 YDS

Incline to Findall
Coal Slope

Layout in 1878 (not to Scale)

HOWBEACH SIDINGS

Opened: 25th May 1868
Closed: 1921 (last train); 1932 (official closure)
Date of survey: 1905

Howbeach Sidings were, after 1878, at the end of the Central line, although track remained to the north until 1911. There was a loop on one side of the running line, from which a siding crossed the road to serve the small Howbeach Colliery. On the other side, an incline ran up the hillside to Findall Coal Slope.

The service was remarkable for its lack of traffic. The 1921 coal strike finished off the pits at Howbeach, and that was that. The line closed north of Blakeney. The GWR did not officially close the line until 1932, and track remained, at least, until 1940, but there was no traffic at all. The line petered out in the middle of nowhere.

For plans of New Fancy Colliery and the end of the line, please refer to the section on the S&W mineral loop.

SECTION 7

NEWNHAM TO CINDERFORD AND DRYBROOK
(SOUTH WALES RAILWAY – GWR)

Known as the Forest of Dean branch, this line was opened by the South Wales Railway on 24th July 1854 to replace the earlier tramway over the same route. Built to the broad gauge, the line ran from Bullo Pill Junction, where a line served a small dock, to Bilson Junction, near Cinderford, and north to terminate at Cinderford Goods, later called Whimsey.

The line was very heavily used, so much so that four engines were kept at Bullo Shed, but passenger traffic was not considered. The gauge was narrowed on 11/12th May 1872 along with the main line. In 1873, the Severn & Wye line made a junction with the branch, north of Bilson, although there was no through running. The GWR had taken over the SWR on 1st August 1863.

Passenger services commenced on the line on 3rd August 1907, resulting in a series of halts opening and trains running into the new S&W Cinderford Station after 1908. The trains ran as far north as Drybrook, on the line built in 1883 north from Whimsey, but not, until now, opened. A bay was put in at Newnham and trains ran to here along the main line. Auto trains were always used.

The branch passenger service ceased on 3rd November 1958, the branch surviving for freight until 1st August 1967.

Opened: 19th September 1851
Closed: 2nd November 1964
Date of survey: 1920

Newnham was, for years, a simple through station on the SWR main line, with two platforms and a single goods siding serving a large stone goods shed.

The start of the GWR passenger service, on the Forest of Dean branch on 3rd August 1907, involved the laying of a bay platform at Newnham, for which the cutting was widened, the extra width left by the broad gauge also being of value. The whole station was in a cutting, and the line entered Newnham Tunnel to the west.

Branch trains ran to Bullo Pill Junction on the main line, serving the short-lived Ruddle Road Halt en route. Trains from Bullo ran 'wrong line' along the main line, there being no crossover at Newnham.

Trains increasingly ran through to Gloucester and less use was made of the bay up to the withdrawal of the service on 3rd November 1958. The station remained open for freight and passengers until 2nd November 1964, the signal box having closed in 1957.

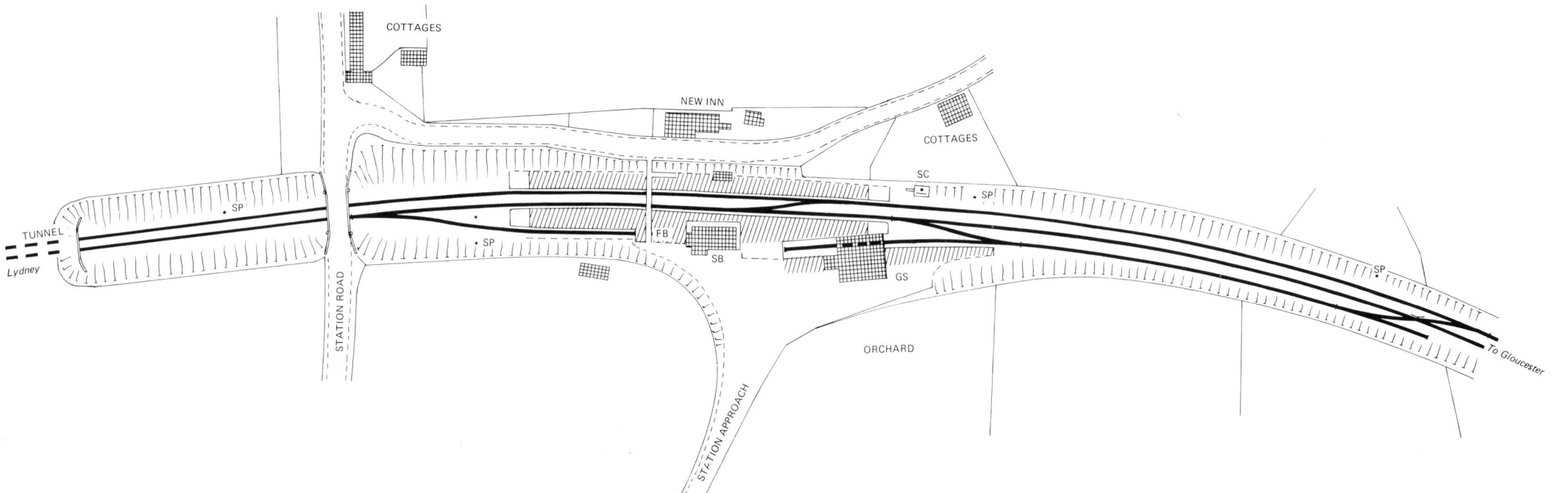

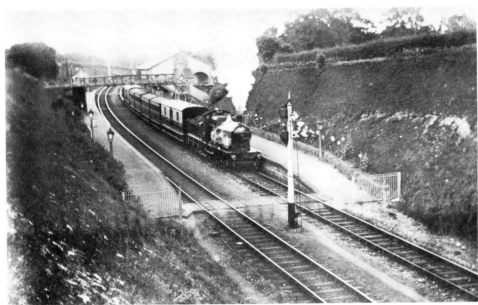

Newnham
A 'down' stopping train at the station. This scene was captured before the bay platform was added in 1907.

Lens of Sutton

Newnham
Ex-GWR 0-4-2T, No. 1409 departs from the bay platform for Cinderford, in 1949.

HMRS

Newnham
Newnham was another station which retained its SWR characteristics right up to the end.

R. Blencowe

Newnham
The Forest rail motor in the bay platform, circa 1910.

Lens of Sutton

BULLO PILL JUNCTION

Opened: 24th July 1854
Closed: 1st August 1967
Date of survey: 1930
Date of signalling plan: circa 1960-1965

Bullo Pill Junction, named after the nearby inlet on the River Severn, came into being with the opening, in 1854, of the Forest of Dean branch as a broad gauge railway, by the SWR. The main line had opened on 19th September 1851.

The junction, sidings and locomotive shed were busy from the start, four broad gauge engines being allocated for the branch and there were two signal boxes.

The GWR took over the SWR on 1st August 1863 and, in 1872, the lines were converted to standard gauge, traffic continuing to build up.

In 1898, two new brick-built signal boxes were opened and, after this date, the layout changed relatively little. The engine shed was closed on 21st March 1931, after which, locomotives came from Gloucester Shed, although the shed building remained for many years. In the 1960s, more drastic contractions took place. The line to Bullo Dock closed on 12th August 1963 and the branch closed to all traffic on 1st August 1967. The West signal box closed on 18th March 1968, and the East box on 2nd June 1969, the site reverting to plain main line.

Bullo Pill Junction
A pannier tank takes on water at the junction in 1964. There were two water tanks at this location, the further one dating from broad gauge days.

B. J. Ashworth

BULLO PILL DOCK

Opened: 1810-1820 (rail connection 24th July 1854)
Closed: Last traffic circa 1926 (rail connection removed 13th October 1963)
Date of survey: 1885

The harbour at Bullo Pill was established from 1810 to 1820 and became the outlet for the Forest of Dean Tramway, although it was never adequate as a port. There was one basin, which was entered through lock gates, and a seperate reservoir to maintain the water level. The tramway served coal tips on both sides of the dock, and traffic was fairly brisk.

When the tramway became a railway in 1854, the SWR built a branch to the dock from Bullo Pill Junction, replacing the tramway.

The branch descended from the junction, serving a wagon works before crossing the dock over a 30ft. span drawbridge, terminating at a deep water riverside wharf. This later handled most traffic. Sidings served two tips and two more sidings stood on the sides of the basin. A works, used originally for building and repairing wagons, was established near the dock, and this continued in use, owned, by then, by Newnham Rubber Mills, after the last barge called in 1926. The dock gates soon collapsed, leaving the dock open to the tides. It quickly silted up. Traffic to the works ceased in 1963 and the overgrown branch line was lifted on 13th October of the same year.

Bullo Cross Halt
Situated just north of the junction, Bullo Cross Halt was opened in 1907.

HMRS

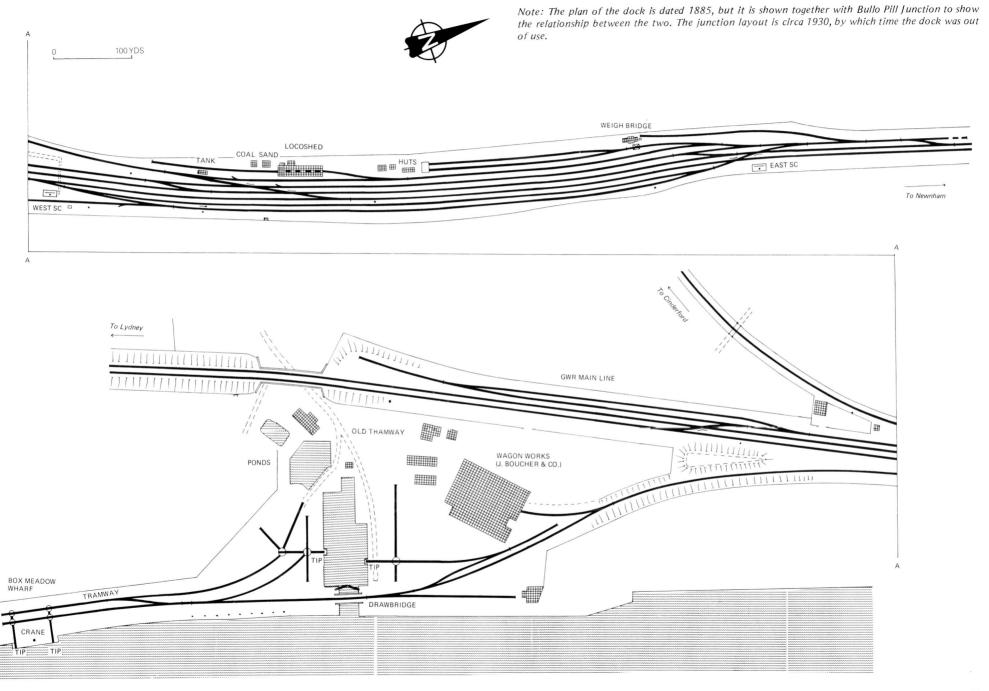

Note: The plan of the dock is dated 1885, but it is shown together with Bullo Pill Junction to show the relationship between the two. The junction layout is circa 1930, by which time the dock was out of use.

0   100 YDS

WEIGH BRIDGE

LOCOSHED

TANK

COAL SAND

HUTS

EAST SC

WEST SC

To Newnham

To Lydney

To Cinderford

GWR MAIN LINE

OLD TRAMWAY

PONDS

WAGON WORKS
(J. BOUCHER & CO.)

TIP

TIP

BOX MEADOW
WHARF

TRAMWAY

DRAWBRIDGE

CRANE

TIP   TIP

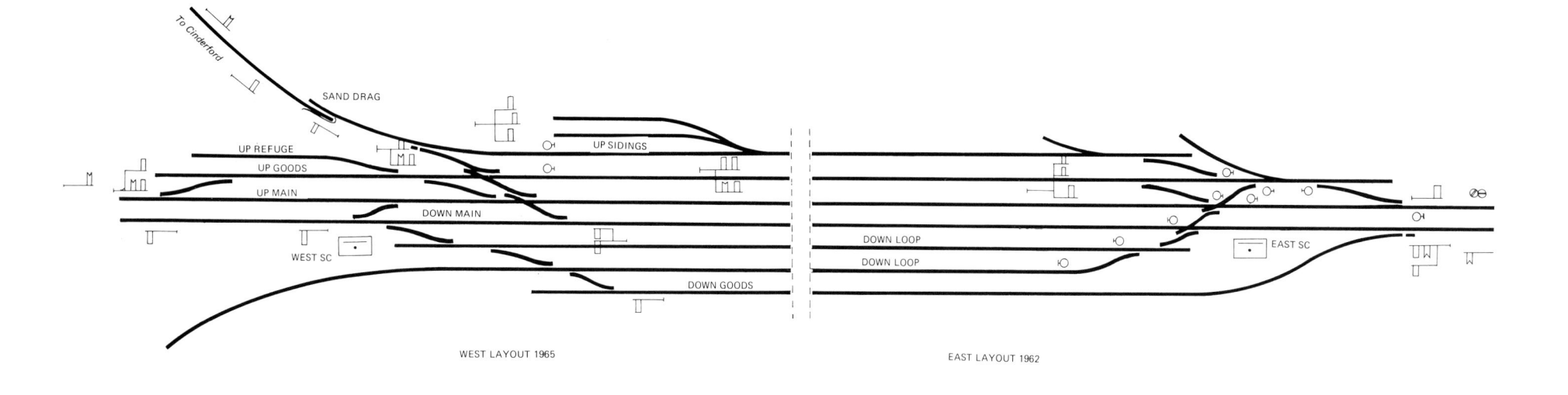

To Cinderford

SAND DRAG

UP REFUGE

UP GOODS

UP MAIN

DOWN MAIN

WEST SC

UP SIDINGS

DOWN LOOP

DOWN LOOP

EAST SC

DOWN GOODS

WEST LAYOUT 1965

EAST LAYOUT 1962

Bullo Engine Shed
A view of the shed building.

Lens of Sutton

Bullo Engine Shed
The shed after closure, seen in use for wagon storage.

L&GRP

Lower Soudley

Ex-GWR 0-6-0PT, No. 8729 passes Lower Soudley with coal empties in April 1962. The site of the ironworks sidings is in the foreground.

B. J. Ashworth

SOUDLEY FURNACE

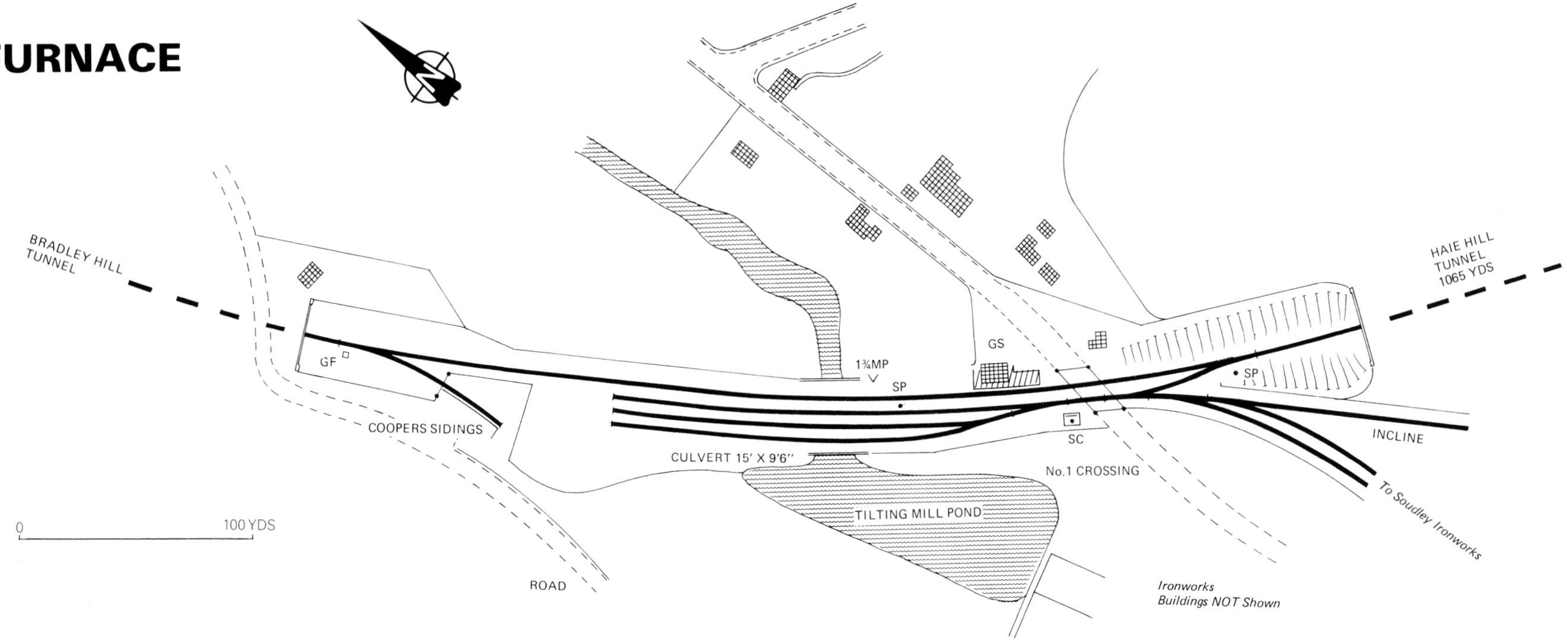

BRADLEY HILL
TUNNEL

HAIE HILL
TUNNEL
1065 YDS

GF

GS

1¾MP

SP

SP

COOPERS SIDINGS

INCLINE

CULVERT 15' X 9'6"

SC

No.1 CROSSING

To Soudley Ironworks

TILTING MILL POND

*Ironworks
Buildings NOT Shown*

0   100 YDS

ROAD

UPPER SOUDLEY

POND

TRACK

POND

HALT

GF

HOUSE

BRADLEY HILL
TUNNEL 299YDS

To Bilson

No.2 CROSSING

To Bullo

UPPER SOUDLEY

POND

STREAM

To Brook F...

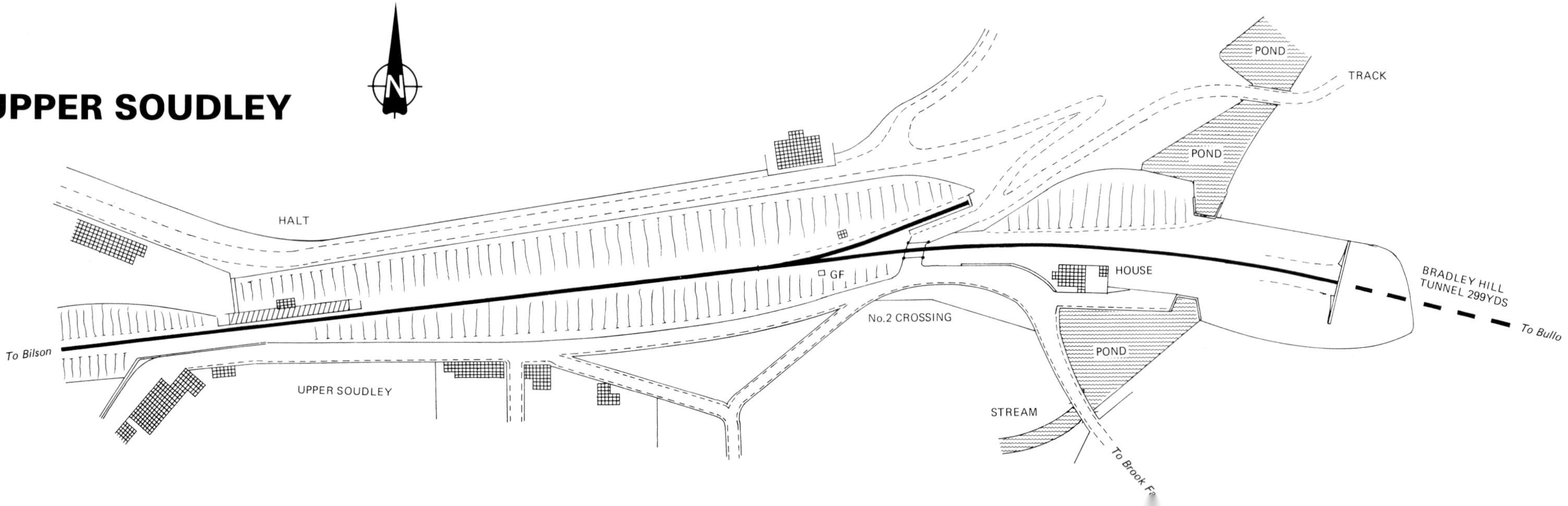

Upper Soudley
Upper Soudley Halt, seen after closure.

R. Blencowe

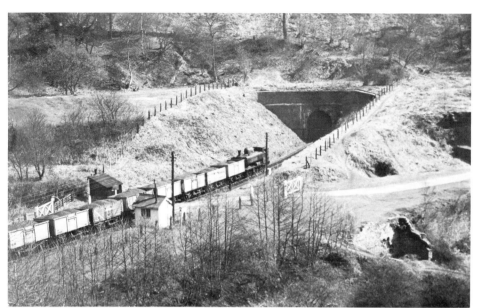

Lower Soudley
Lower Soudley, with the entrance to Haic Hill Tunnel. A train of Forest coal heads south. The remains of the old ironworks are on the right.

B. J. Ashworth

Soudley
Soudley No. 1 Crossing ground frame cabin.

S. Clarkson

Upper Soudley
The overgrown platform, sometime after closure.

Lens of Sutton

UPPER SOUDLEY AND SOUDLEY FURNACE

Opened: 24th July 1854 (Line); 3rd August 1907 (Halt)
Closed: 1st August 1967 (Line): 3rd November 1958 (Halt)
Date of survey: 1910

The GWR branch ran through a succession of tunnels north of Bullo, and between the portals of Haie Hill and Bradley Hill tunnels was a siding serving Soudley Ironworks. Dating back to broad gauge days, the sidings were worked by the works' own small locomotive. By 1875, the works was known as the Great Western Ironworks. A signal box opened in 1907, but the sidings were out of use by 1920, and were removed.

Opposite the signal box stood a little goods shed, a rare example of loading directly from the running line. Just before Bradley Hill Tunnel was a small gated siding, named Coopers Sidings, at which coal was loaded.

The tunnel, 299 yards in length, was followed by another small spur, Soudley Siding, serving a wharf. This was rarely used. Beyond, was Upper Soudley Halt, opened in 1907 and consisting of a wooden fronted platform with the usual pagoda hut. It was well placed to serve the village in the valley bottom, as were most halts along this route.

STAPLE EDGE AND EASTERN UNITED COLLIERY

Opened: 3rd August 1907 (Halt); 14th December 1913 (Colliery)
Closed: 3rd November 1958 (Halt); January 1959 (Colliery)
Date of survey: 1920

The line approached Staple Edge on a sharp curve. Just before the road bridge, which was situated south of the halt, a long loop siding served Shakemantle Colliery, a small concern, which, for many years, had no road access. The siding was in use as early as 1856, also serving an iron mine and lime kilns. In 1962, after years of disuse, it was removed.

The line curved sharply to run under the road bridge and past Eastern United Colliery, on the left of the line. Served by extensive sidings, the pit was opened in December 1913 and remained one of the largest producers in the area until closure in 1959. A signal box controlled the sidings and the loop, opposite which stood Staple Edge Halt, a usual single platform, which was opened in 1907.

Staple Edge
A view from the road bridge, in 1964.

R. Blencowe

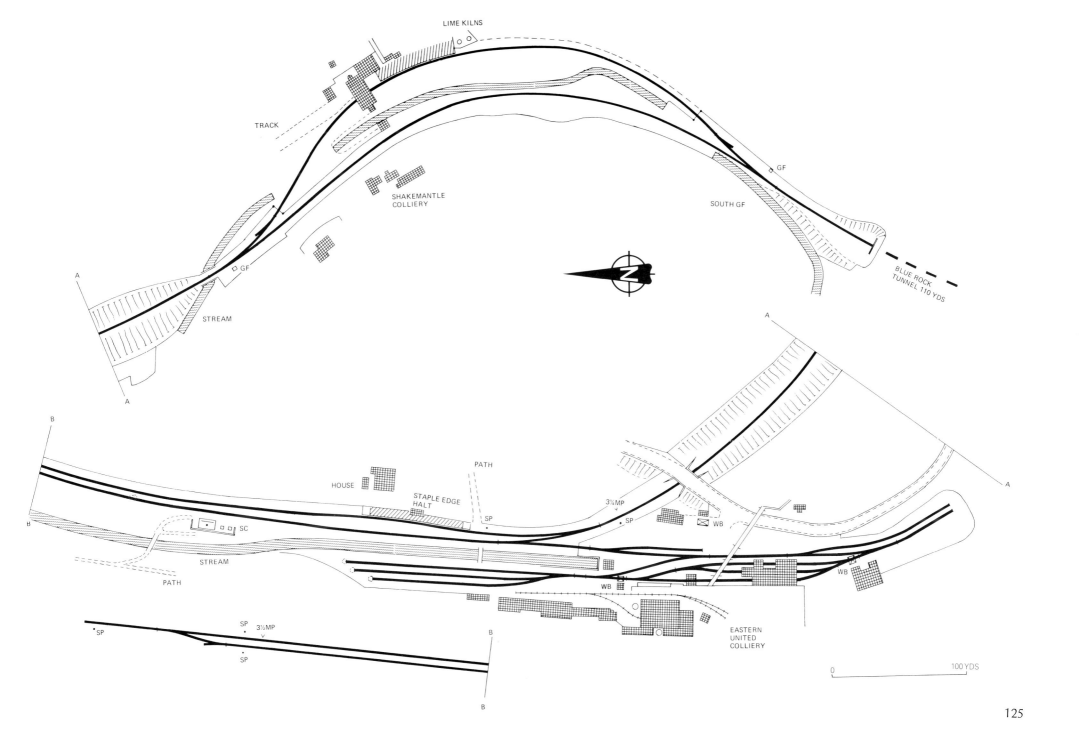

LIME KILNS

TRACK

SHAKEMANTLE
COLLIERY

GF

SOUTH GF

BLUE ROCK
TUNNEL 110 YDS

GF

A

STREAM

A

A

A

B

PATH

HOUSE

STAPLE EDGE
HALT

3¼MP

B

SC

SP

SP

WB

STREAM

PATH

WB

WB

SP

3½MP

SP

EASTERN
UNITED
COLLIERY

B

SP

B

0   100 YDS

125

RUSPIDGE HALT

Opened: 3rd August 1907
Closed: 3rd November 1958
Date of survey: 1910

Ruspidge was situated just north of the level crossing by which the main Cinderford to Coleford road crossed the branch, and was the only halt to have a proper building and platform. Ruspidge boasted a small stone-built building and opposite this, there was a goods shed which was served by a single siding. Presumably, the station, when opened, was meant to serve parts of Cinderford, although the new Cinderford Station had been open for seven years to S&W trains. The siding was out of use long before closure of the halt in 1958.

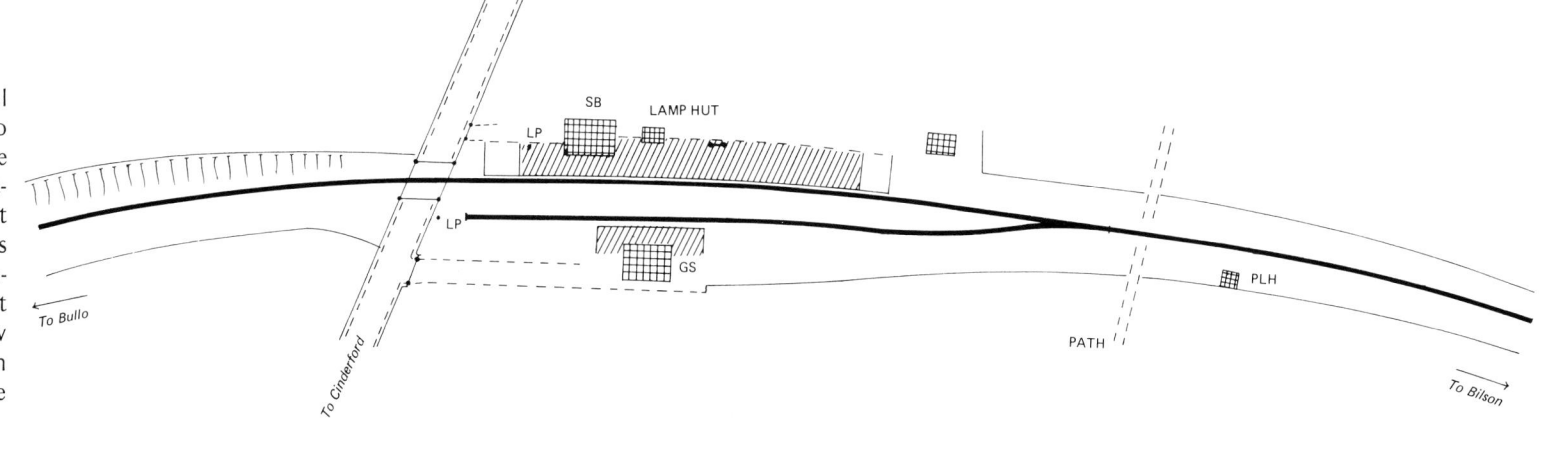

0   100 YDS

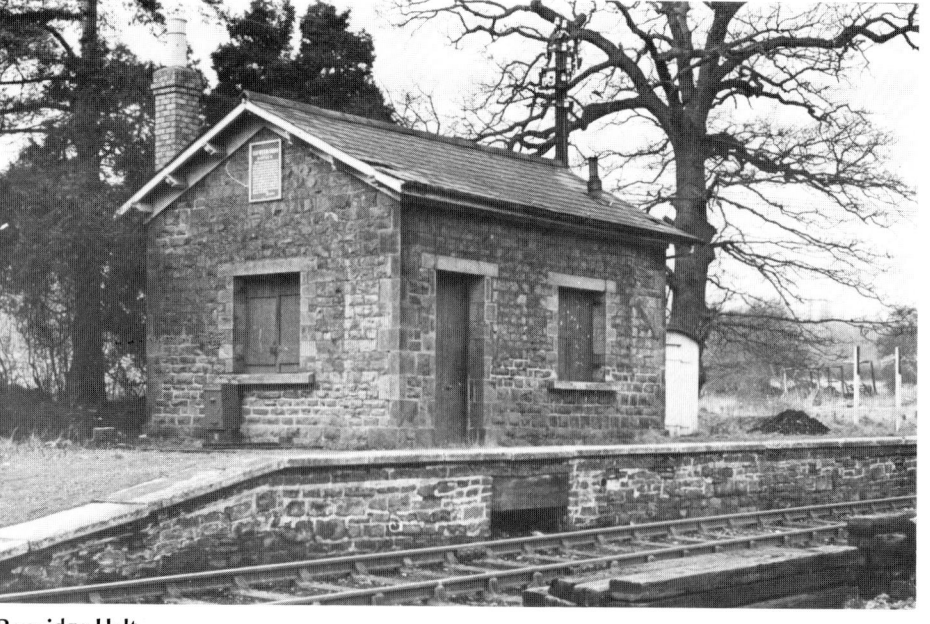

Ruspidge Halt
The station building.

S. Clarkson

Ruspidge Halt
A coal empties train heads north, through the station, in 1965.

B. J. Ashworth

RUSPIDGE STATION BUILDING

The station building at Ruspidge Halt was a small stone structure with a slated roof, comprising a waiting-room and an office. The three windows, unusually, had shutters, but otherwise there was little to note about the building.

Its design resembled those built by the SWR on the main line, such as Awre Junction, leading to speculation that it preceded the opening of the line, to passengers, in 1907. It may originally have been a goods office. Had it been built in 1907, it seems likely that the GWR would have simply used a standard design, or a pagoda hut, as they had elsewhere on the line. Unfortunately, the facts cannot be confirmed.

Ruspidge Halt
A view of the station, looking north.

Lens of Sutton

Ruspidge Halt
A view, looking south, towards the crossing gates.

Lens of Sutton

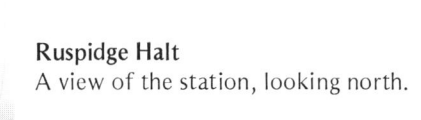

BILSON

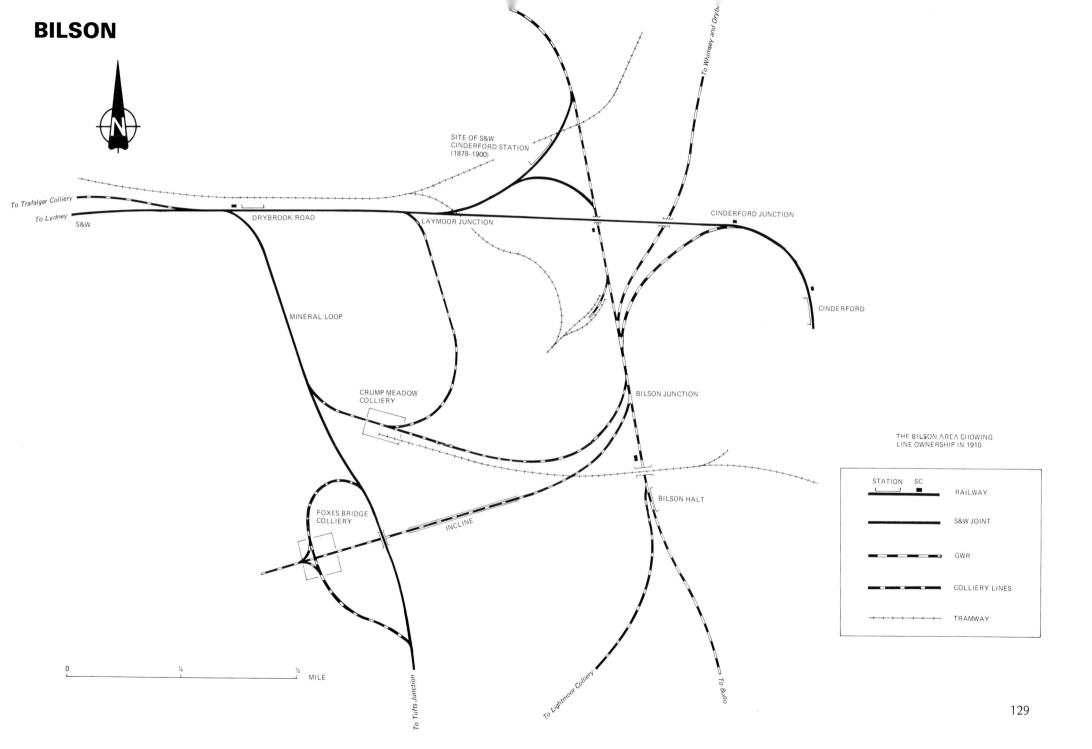

To Trafalgar Colliery
To Lydney
S&W

DRYBROOK ROAD

SITE OF S&W
CINDERFORD STATION
(1878-1900)

To Whimsey and Drybrook

LAYMOOR JUNCTION

CINDERFORD JUNCTION

CINDERFORD

MINERAL LOOP

CRUMP MEADOW
COLLIERY

BILSON JUNCTION

FOXES BRIDGE
COLLIERY

INCLINE

BILSON HALT

To Tufts Junction

To Lightmoor Colliery

To Bullo

THE BILSON AREA SHOWING
LINE OWNERSHIP IN 1910

STATION	SC	
		RAILWAY
		S&W JOINT
		GWR
		COLLIERY LINES
		TRAMWAY

0   ¼   ½   MILE

129

BILSON JUNCTION

Opened: 24th July 1854
Closed: 1st August 1967
Dates of surveys: (1) Map of area, 1875-1878
(2) Map of the area in 1910, showing line ownership
(3) Plan of Bilson Junction, 1920

Bilson Junction was the yard where trains were assembled before beginning the journey down to Bullo Pill and beyond. It was the focal point of many colliery lines, the junction for the S&W line, and also, after 1908, for Cinderford, and the story of its development is a little complicated and, therefore, three plans are provided. Reference should also be made to the relevent plans in the S&W section, such as Cinderford and Crump Meadow Colliery.

The original line of 1854 ran through the junction to terminate at Cinderford Goods, or Whimsey, a little to the north, while a branch ran off to serve collieries in the Churchway area, forming the beginnings of the junction. Sidings were provided where the two lines met. The Churchway line also formed an interchange with the S&W Tramway.

There were many collieries in the area and, within a few years of opening, lines had been built to serve Lightmoor, Foxes Bridge and Crump Meadow pits, plus an interchange wharf with the tramway from Trafalgar Colliery. The Foxes Bridge line was worked via a rope-operated self balancing incline. All the colliery lines were privately owned, but only the Lightmoor line was worked by the colliery company.

With all these lines feeding traffic into Bilson Junction, the yard soon became the busiest place on the Forest railway system, with trains of 100 wagons departing for Bullo on occasions.

Little changed until 1873, when the newly-converted S&W Railway arrived, forming a junction north of Bilson on the Churchway line. The first plan shows the area during this period, from 1875-1878, when the S&W's Bilson Platform was in use. The S&W station was opened in 1878, and is dealt with separately. Many of the tramways remained in use during this period.

The next change came in 1900, when the new S&W Joint Committee opened the extension of the S&W to the new Cinderford Station, crossing the GWR on an embankment to the north of the junction. In 1907, the GWR introduced a passenger service to Drybrook, a halt opening south of Bilson Junction. It boasted two pagoda huts, reflecting the expected traffic, but this never materialized. Trains ran through to Drybrook, on an extension of the Whimsey line, and on 6th April 1908, a loop was opened, allowing trains to use Cinderford Station. This involved demolition of Bilson goods shed. Trains ran into Cinderford and reversed back to Bilson before continuing their journeys. A new twenty three lever signal box was opened and a siding was laid to stable the auto train when it was not in use. Bilson Halt was closed, but reopened on 2nd April 1917, finally closing on 1st October 1920.

The second map shows the whole area as it was in 1920, with the ownership of the various lines, while the scale plan shows Bilson Junction itself, in 1920, the other sections being covered separately. A few colliery connections had been removed, but traffic was still brisk.

The decline of the area set in soon after 1920, the Crump Meadow branch being removed when the pit closed in 1929, with Foxes Bridge closing around the same time. The Lightmoor line lasted until 8th June 1940. In 1951, the connections with the S&W were removed when that line was closed, and the S&W junction ground frame was removed. This was a small gable-roofed wooden building, similar to a small signal box. The S&W line to Cinderford was closed and the bridges over the GWR line were removed. Passenger trains remained until 1958 and, by this time, the yard was quiet, used mainly by coal trains from Northern United Pit on the Churchway line. When the pit closed in 1967, so did the branch, on 1st August. Little now remains of Bilson Junction to show the importance it once had on the Forest's railway system.

Bilson Junction
An overall view of the general layout as seen from the Crump Meadow Tramway embankment.

B. J. Ashworth

BILSON

TRAFALGAR TRAMWAY

S&W

G.W.R.

To Whimsey GWR

LC

BILSON PLATFORM

SC

SIDING

0   350 YDS

THE BILSON AREA, 1875-1878

BILSON GREEN

CRUMP MEADOW
TRAMWAY

BILSON JUNCTION

N

To Ironworks

SC

To Crump Meadow Colliery

WB

GS

To Lightmoor Colliery

To Bullo

To Foxes Bridge Colliery

Bilson Junction
A pannier tank runs past the site of the junction which once ran to Cinderford.

B. J. Ashworth

BILSON JUNCTION

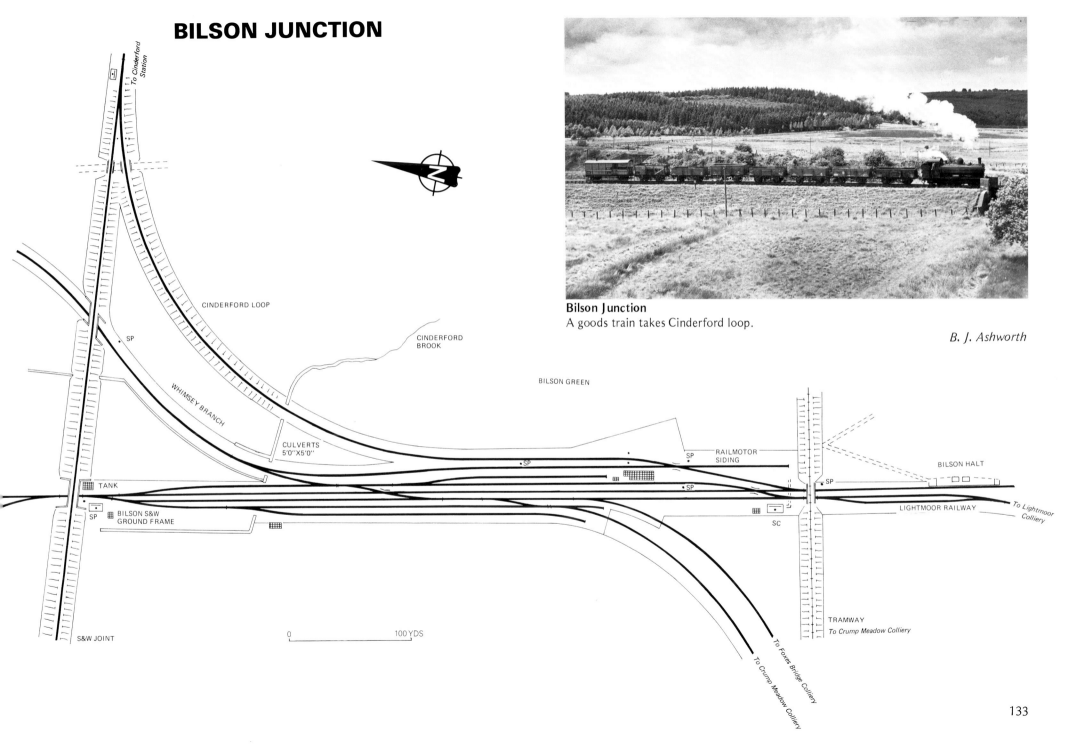

To Cinderford Station

CINDERFORD LOOP

CINDERFORD BROOK

SP

WHIMSEY BRANCH

CULVERTS 5'0"X5'0"

BILSON GREEN

TANK

SP

BILSON S&W GROUND FRAME

SP

RAILMOTOR SIDING

BILSON HALT

SP

SP

SP

LIGHTMOOR RAILWAY

To Lightmoor Colliery

SC

S&W JOINT

TRAMWAY
To Crump Meadow Colliery

To Foxes Bridge Colliery

To Crump Meadow Colliery

0   100 YDS

Bilson Junction
A goods train takes Cinderford loop.

B. J. Ashworth

133

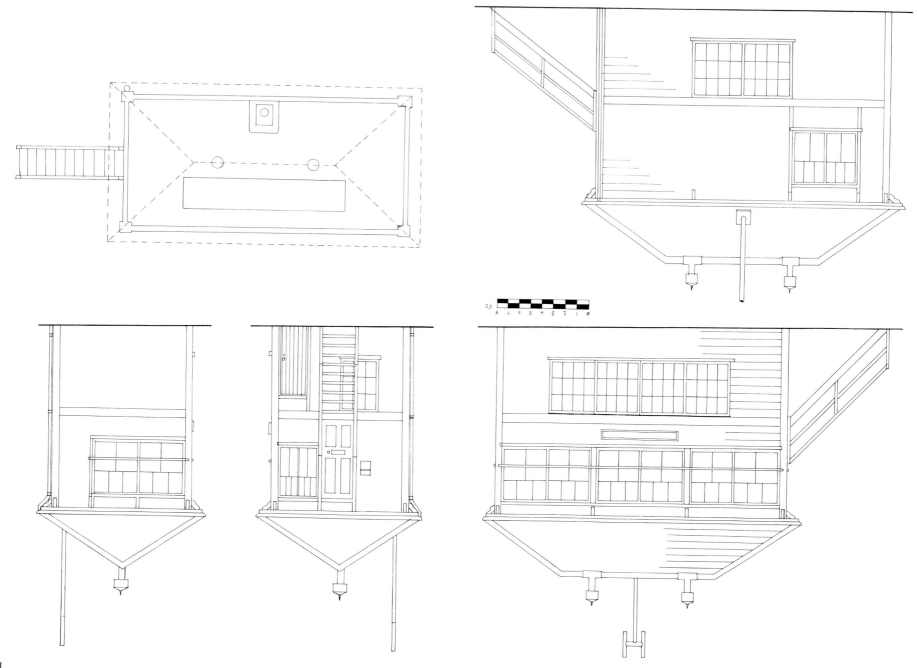

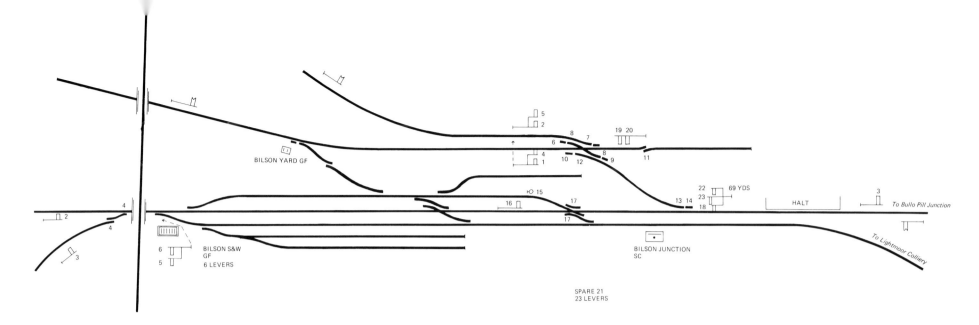

BILSON JUNCTION

BILSON YARD GF

5
2

8 7   19 20

6

4   10 12   8
1   9   11

22   69 YDS
23

15   HALT   3
                                                    To Bullo Pill Junction

2

4   16   17

4   17

6   BILSON S&W   13 14
         GF   18
5   6 LEVERS

3   BILSON JUNCTION
                     SC

To Lightmoor Colliery

SPARE 21
23 LEVERS

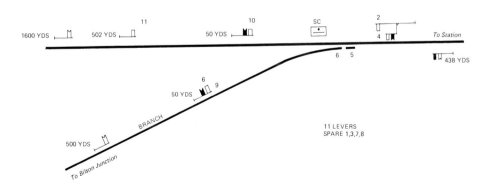

1600 YDS   502 YDS   11   10   SC   2
                                      50 YDS   4

                                                          To Station

                                    6 5

                                    438 YDS

                    6
500 YDS   50 YDS   9

BRANCH

11 LEVERS
SPARE 1,3,7,8

To Bilson Junction

135

Bilson Junction
A freight train prepares for the journey to Bullo.

B. J. Ashworth

Bilson Junction
A freight train descends the loop line from Cinderford. The Whimsey line is seen in the foreground. The photograph was taken from the S & W embankment.

B. J. Ashworth

Bilson Junction
The junction in 1961.

S. Clarkson

WHIMSEY

Opened: 24th July 1854 (Goods Station); 3rd August 1907 (Halt)
Closed: 2nd May 1967 (Goods Station); 7th July 1930 (Halt)
Date of survey: 1925

Whimsey was the end of the Forest of Dean branch from its opening in 1854, and a goods station was opened there to serve Cinderford, thereby reducing congestion at Bilson Junction. The line north of the junction also served several small collieries.

The line was extended to the north of Whimsey, in July 1885, for freight trains to Speedwell Siding as part of the Mitcheldean Road & Forest of Dean Junction Railway; an ill-fated scheme inherited by the GWR. The line was extended to Drybrook for the start of passenger services on 3rd August 1907, at which time a halt was opened to serve Whimsey.

The goods station was extended in 1925, and a siding at the rear was added. Passenger trains ceased in 1930 and the line north of Whimsey finally closed in February 1953. In 1949, the firm of Berry Wiggins had taken over part of the goods station as a depot for their bitumen tankers. This traffic continued until 1967 when the depot was transferred to Lydney. This having been the only traffic, the line closed north of Bilson on 2nd May 1967.

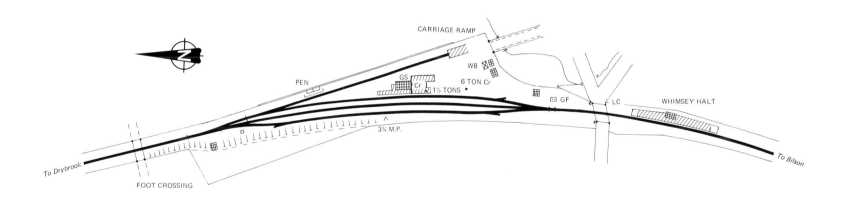

CARRIAGE RAMP

PEN

GS

Cr

1½ TONS

6 TON Cr

WB

GF

LC

WHIMSEY HALT

3¾ M.P.

To Drybrook

FOOT CROSSING

To Bilson

0   100 YDS

A pannier tank shunts wagons just north of the Berry Wiggins depot. The line was severed beyond here.

B. J. Ashworth

Whimsey
Tankers from Berry Wiggins depot head south for Bilson Junction, and pass the old S & W
embankment.

B. J. Ashworth

DRYBROOK

HAWTHORNS TUNNEL
634 YDS

STREAM

TRAMWAY

HALT

To Whimsey

0   100 YDS

STEAM MILLS CROSSING

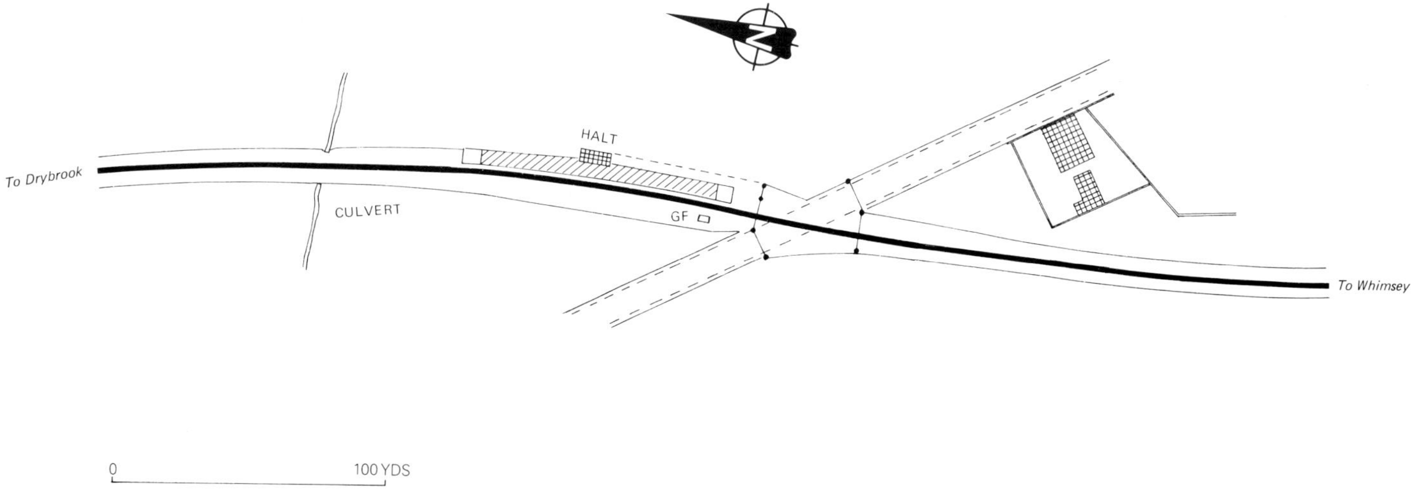

To Whimsey

To Drybrook

CULVERT

GF

HALT

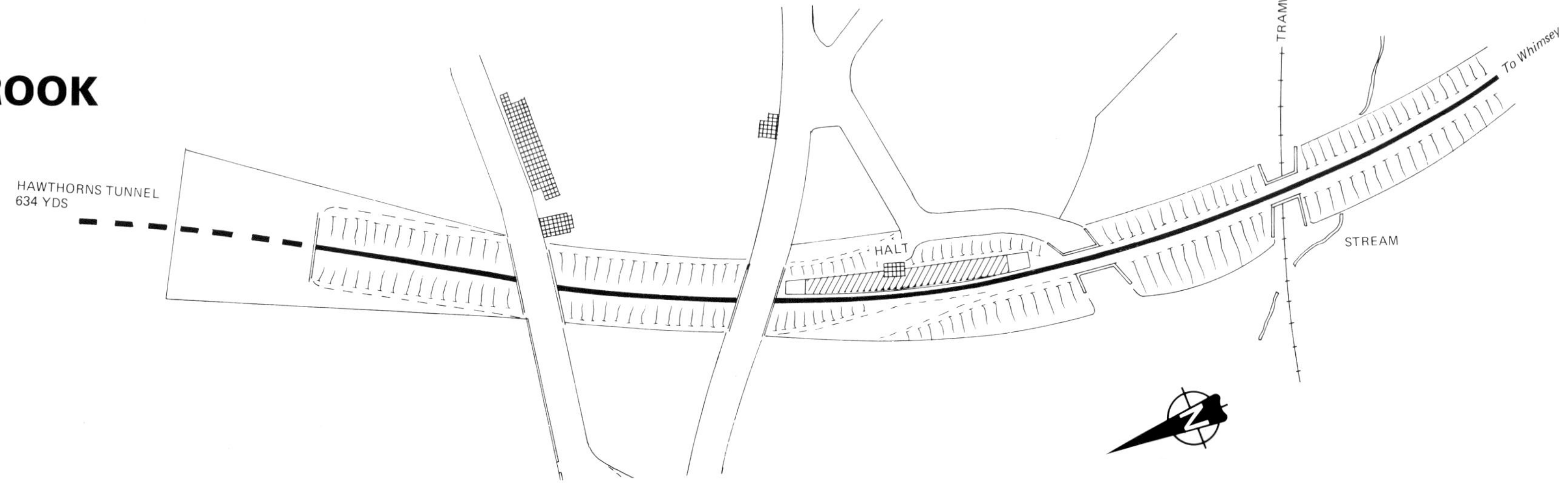

Drybrook
A view looking along the formation to Drybrook Tunnel.

S. Clarkson

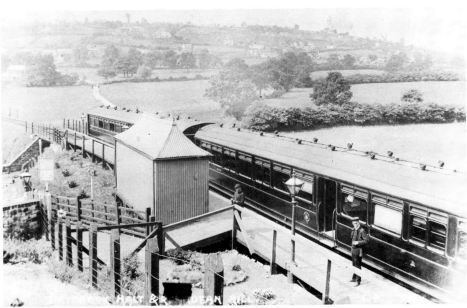

Drybrook
Drybrook Station, as seen from the road bridge, soon after the service began. The coaches seem to be in crimson lake livery.

Lens of Sutton

Drybrook
A bridge at Nailbridge, between Steam Mills and Drybrook. Beyond, is the original tramway bridge.

S. Clarkson

Drybrook
A view from the site of the halt, showing both bridges.

S. Clarkson

Steam Mills Crossing
A train at the halt, soon after its opening.

Lens of Sutton

STEAM MILLS CROSSING AND DRYBROOK HALTS

Opened: 3rd August 1907 (Steam Mills); 4th November 1907 (Drybrook)
Closed: 7th July 1930
Date of survey: 1910

The passenger service as far north as Steam Mills Crossing Halt began on 3rd August 1907 from Newnham, the journey taking half an hour. The extension to Drybrook Halt came on 4th November of that year, this being the northern passenger terminus until the withdrawal of the service in 1930.

The halts were of the usual wooden platform/pagoda combination, and the trains were always auto trailers coupled to an 0-6-0T or 0-4-2T engine. The line was opened north of Drybrook Halt, to a quarry, on 18th October 1928, but the section from there to Mitcheldean Road never saw traffic of any kind.

Following the closure to passengers, freight traffic declined until the line was closed, having had very little use, in February 1953.

The gradient post at the summit of the S&W's Coleford branch.

R. Blencowe

Ex-GWR 0-6-0PT, No. 1664 hauls a brake van special between Lydney and Severn Bridge on 20th June 1964.

R. Blencowe

Ex-GWR 0-6-0PT, No. 9616 stands at Lydney Junction with a shunters truck branded 'Lydney S&W Joint'.

R. Blencowe

The brake van special, seen further north, approaching Coleford Junction from Speech House Road.

R. Blencowe

Moseley Green Tunnel, on the mineral loop line.

P. Copeland

Northern United Colliery, which was closed in 1965. This was the last large Forest colliery.

R. Blencowe

The bridge built for the mineral loop to cross the Central line. However, this was not completed and the central line never reached this point.

P. Copeland